The
Reference Shelf®

UFOs

The Reference Shelf
Volume 94 • Number 1
H.W. Wilson
A Division of EBSCO Information Services, Inc.

Published by
GREY HOUSE PUBLISHING
Amenia, New York
2022

The Reference Shelf

The books in this series contain reprints of articles, excerpts from books, addresses on current issues, and studies of social trends in the United States and other countries. There are six separately bound numbers in each volume, all of which are usually published in the same calendar year. Numbers one through five are each devoted to a single subject, providing background information and discussion from various points of view and concluding with an index and comprehensive bibliography that lists books, pamphlets, and articles on the subject. The final number of each volume is a collection of recent speeches. Books in the series may be purchased individually or on subscription.

Publisher's Cataloging-In-Publication Data
(Prepared by The Donohue Group, Inc.)

Names: Grey House Publishing, Inc., compiler.
Title: UFOs / [compiled by Grey House Publishing].
Other Titles: Reference shelf ; v. 94, no. 1.
Description: Amenia, New York : Grey House Publishing, 2022. | Includes bibliographical references and index.
Identifiers: ISBN 9781637002919 (v. 94, no. 1) | ISBN 9781637002902 (volume set)
Subjects: LCSH: Unidentified flying objects--United States--Sources. | Life on other planets--Sources. | Extraterrestrial beings--Sources. | Human-alien encounters--United States--Sources.
Classification: LCC TL789.4 .U36 2022 | DDC 001.9420973--dc23

Printed in Canada

Contents

5

The View from Above

Those Who Want to Believe

Aliens in Popular Culture

Aliens and UFOs are part of mainstream popular culture in the United States. Each year, books, movies, and television series provide ever more nuanced and varied explorations of aliens and alien visitation. This enormous popularity reflects many aspects of human culture and storytelling, with artists in a variety of media using aliens and alien visitation to critique and celebrate human life as well as to speculate about the nature of the universe and the possibilities for humanity's future.

While the artists who tell extraterrestrial stories take their inspiration from a variety of places, the "true" stories of alien visitation, UFO sightings, and alien abductions have played a major role in shaping pop-cultural depictions of aliens and UFOs. The stories and legends of alleged alien visitors has homogenized the image of alien life in popular culture to the point that even a simple emoji-style illustration of a large-eyed green or gray head is immediately recognizable to children and adults alike as an "alien." To some, the similarities in the way people imagine UFOs and aliens is proof that real experiences and real sightings have occurred, creating a shared vision of alien activity, but skeptics argue that these shared ideas and images demonstrate how ideas spread through cultures and also reflect the degree to which Americans continue to be fascinated by the possibility of life beyond the limitations of the Earth.

History of Alien Mystery

Humans have been theorizing about life on other planets since before recorded history, and many of the oldest and most enduring myths were inspired, in part, by theories about lights in the skies and their origins. As humanity advanced technologically, so too did the human imagination about fantastic future or extraterrestrial technology that might exist somewhere out in the universe. Fascination with aliens and alien visitation was in many ways a reflection of American fascination with technology itself and with the possibility of new frontiers of exploration and discovery.

However, the idea that aliens and UFOs might actually exist did not gain mainstream popularity until the 1940s. High-profile incidents involving alleged UFO sightings, such as the 1947 recovery of weather balloon debris in Roswell, New Mexico, helped to create the perception that UFOs might actually be visiting the Earth. Stories like those surrounding the Roswell incident, combined with sightings of real-life prototype aircraft that had been developed in secret military facilities, gave rise to the idea that perhaps government scientists had already made secret contact with UFOs. UFO enthusiasts fascinated by the classified research going on in secret government flight facilities manufactured many stories and theories about captive aliens and alien technology allegedly hidden within these facilities. Over the years, and for reasons that often remain unknown, many people claimed to have seen aliens or alien technology concealed by government agents and, by the mid-1950s, the idea of secret government UFO research was well established in the popular imagination.

By the 1960s, UFOs and aliens were already familiar themes in science fiction and in American pop culture in general, but the imagery of alien life was much more diverse than it would become in subsequent decades. One of the factors that helped to create a common stereotype of alien visitation were stories of "alien abduction," which became a popular subgenre of alien fiction in the 1960s. The popularity of alien abduction stories can be traced to articles, books, and a movie describing the alleged experiences of Barney and Betty Hill, who claimed they had been abducted while driving along a mountain road in New Hampshire in 1961. The Hills said they had been taken aboard an alien craft where they met a group of small, gray-skinned aliens with large teardrop-shaped heads and big, almond-shaped eyes. These aliens conducted medical experiments on the couple, including taking samples of reproductive material allegedly to conduct "breeding experiments," before returning the couple to earth. The Hills described the aliens as friendly and believed that their intentions had been good, providing the overall impression of these short, gray aliens as scientists interested in studying humanity, but not harboring any perceptively dangerous or malicious intentions.

Faith in the Unknown

By the 1970s, American UFO mythos was well established in a form similar to what exists in the twenty-first century. Sightings of weather balloons, confidential aircraft, and a variety of other strange physical phenomenon helped to inspire and maintain the belief that strangely shaped alien vehicles had visited Earth. Then, stories of alien abductions, many similar to the stories told by the Hills, helped to create the stereotyped alien image: a green or gray creature, typically thin and shorter than the average human, with an oversized teardrop-shaped head and big eyes, who flew in disk- or saucer-like aircraft. Another major pillar of UFO belief involves the idea that the government (1) knows more about aliens than is generally known, and/or (2) has already made contact with aliens or has remnants of alien bodies and/or alien technology kept in secret locations. Finally, the third major prong of Ufology is the idea that aliens have abducted humans for scientific purposes and therefore that aliens are either explorers studying humanity or perhaps are experimenting with humans and studying human reproduction for some unknown purpose.

From the beginning, the line between alien fiction and alien fact was blurry and, as common stories about alien visitation and UFOs became popular themes in fiction, these stories inspired myths and legends of allegedly real alien encounters, which then inspired more fiction about aliens and UFOs, etc. The problem with belief in UFOs and alien visitation is that no solid evidence has ever been found, despite the fact that advancements in technology have meant that more and more Americans have been able to join in the "hunt" for extraterrestrial technology and visitors. Outside of the many thousands of scientists studying the night sky with telescopes, satellites, and other tools, there is an army of tens of thousands of amateur astronomers and space enthusiasts who likewise contribute to what is essentially one of the most massive surveillance operations of all time. On any given night, thousands of Americans are scanning the night sky for signs of planets, comets or other cosmic phenomena, and many of these people—from scientists or specialists to amateur astronomers—are specifically looking for signs of UFOs and alien visitors, fascinated by the remote possibility of glimpsing signs of life outside the solar system.

Because this vast and growing web of surveillance has been unable to find any physical evidence to justify belief in UFO visitation, belief in UFOs and alien visitors is largely a matter of faith. Existing "evidence" of alien encounters and extraterrestrial visitation hinges on first-person accounts and testimonials, which are notoriously untrustworthy because humans are inherently vulnerable to misperception. When a person sees, hears, or feels something that they cannot understand, imagination comes into play as the person tries to make sense of the phenomenon. If the person already believes in supernatural phenomenon like ghosts, they might perceive audio or visual hallucinations or illusions as evidence of a haunting. If a person believes, or wants to believe, in UFOs and alien visitation, they might perceive any cosmic illusion, flashing light, or other unexplained aerial phenomenon as a UFO.

Stories of unexplained sightings, increasingly coupled with video and photographic evidence, help to encourage belief in extraterrestrial visitation even though none of the encounters ever described—whether involving citizens traveling alone on rural roads or naval pilots encountering strange aircraft in the sky—have ever provided enough evidence to suggest alien technology has ever come to Earth. What the existing data does show, however, is that the sky is filled with phenomena that are difficult to explain and that even with the advanced technology available to humanity, there are many mysteries that still remain to be discovered through scientific investigation.

There is another factor that helps to maintain belief in UFOs, and this is that many scientists and astronomers have expressed their belief that there is a statistical likelihood that alien life exists somewhere in the universe. This does not mean that many mainstream scientists or experts in the field believe that alien spacecraft have visited the Earth, or that aliens have been captured by the military, or that aliens abduct humans for scientific purposes. Rather, scientific exploration of the cosmos coupled with our deepening understanding of the universe has convinced many scientists that alien life is likely to exist somewhere, in some form, in some part of the universe. There is far less agreement among specialists with regard to the idea that aliens' organisms would be able or have been able to visit the Earth, and few astronomers and other types of space scientists believe that aliens have already visited or have abducted humans. The science of UFOs involves investigating the types of technology that would be needed for interstellar travel and searching the cosmos for signs of planets capable of supporting life. There are overlaps between mainstream UFO interest and the scientific investigations of possible alien life (exobiology), and research has stimulated and influenced mainstream pop-cultural perceptions and fantasies about aliens and UFOs as well.

Who Wants to Believe?

Gallup began asking Americans whether UFOs were "something real" or "just people's imagination" in 1973. The organization continued to ask this question in annual studies over the decades that followed. In 1978, Gallup saw a spike in belief, with 57 percent believing that UFOs were real, while in 1990 the Gallup poll found that only 47 percent believed the same. In 2019, Gallup asked this question again and found that belief in UFOs had climbed back to late 1970s levels, with 56 percent stating that UFOs were real, while 39 percent believed they were imagined.[1]

Many early polls simply asked whether UFOs were real, and not whether UFO sightings represented alien visitation. Other opinion polls have attempted to obtain more detail on American belief by differentiating between potential origins. A 2019 Quinnipiac poll, for instance, found that 42 percent of Americans believed that UFO sightings represented aircraft that had been built by humans, whereas 35 percent believed that UFO sightings indicated extraterrestrial visitors.[2] Likewise, the Roper Starch Worldwide research firm asked about UFOs on several occasions between the 1970s and the 2010s and found that in 1977 only 29 percent of Americans believed that UFOs came from other planets, even while Gallup polling revealed that more than half of Americans believed in UFOs.[3]

Recent research from Pew Research Center indicates that around 65 percent of Americans believe that intelligent life exists beyond the Earth, while 51 percent believe that UFO reports might be evidence of extraterrestrial life, compared to 47 percent who believe that UFO sightings and reports are probably not evidence of extraterrestrial life. However, Pew polling also indicates that Americans do not, in general, consider UFOs to be a major security threat or a significant cause for concern, even if such sightings do indicate extraterrestrial visitors.[4] The most recent Gallup polls found similar results, but found that belief in alien visitation was still not at majority levels, with approximately 41 percent believing that UFOs involve alien spacecraft, an increase of nearly 10 percentage points from 2019, when only 33 percent believed that UFOs indicated alien origins.[5]

Belief in UFOs and in the possibility that these strange phenomena indicate alien visitation have shifted considerably over time, but only within a relatively narrow range. Since the 1970s, between 40 and 65 percent of Americans believe that UFO sightings are not simply a matter of imagination but represent some kind of real phenomenon. In general, fewer than half of Americans believe that aliens have already visited the United States, but belief in alien visitation has reached a new peak in the 2020s with the release of previously classified UFO videos by the military and discussion of UFOs at the highest levels of politics indicating, to some, that new information on the topic has become available.

Ultimately, though new information on UFO sightings was made available in the recent Pentagon report on government UFO data (released in June of 2021), there is still insufficient data to claim that UFO visitation has occurred, and belief in UFOs is still a matter of faith and, to a large degree, desire.

The seminal American television program *X-Files* told the story of a world in which UFO visitation was a real occurrence and in which aliens had been involved in secret experiments with humans for many years, potentially even centuries. In the show, one of the two main protagonists, Agent Fox Mulder, a UFO believer, has a poster hanging over his desk featuring a blurry image of a flying saucer above the words "I Want to Believe." The poster was an original creation for the series, utilizing an image taken in Europe by a man named Billy Meier and a single, bold line of text inspired by the artwork of Ed Ruscha, and it became an iconic emblem not only of the show but also in the real world of Ufology.[6] The idea that UFO belief is based on a desire to believe speaks to the actual phenomenon of belief in alien abduction and UFO visitation. Belief in alien abduction, UFOs, and alien visitation is not a matter of pure logic and is not a conclusion that can be reached by examining evidence but must depend on an underlying desire to believe. This is especially true when it comes to belief about extrasolar life, because such beliefs often reflect deeper reflections about the meaning of life in the universe and of the possibilities for humanity's future. Believing in alien life suggests new frontiers for exploration, new amazing mysteries awaiting discovery, and also the possibility of a broader future for humanity beyond the limitations of Earth.

Works Used

Bowman, Karlyn, and Andrew Rugg. "Public Opinion on Conspiracy Theories." *AEI*. Nov. 2013. Retrieved from https://www.aei.org/wp-content/uploads/2013/11/-public-opinion-on-conspiracy-theories_181649218739.pdf?x91208.

Kennedy, Courtney, and Arnold Lau. "Most Americans Believe in Intelligent Life Beyond Earth: Few See UFOs as a Major National Security Threat." *Pew Research*. June 30, 2021. Retrieved from https://www.pewresearch.org/fact-tank/2021/06/30/most-americans-believe-in-intelligent-life-beyond-earth-few-see-ufos-as-a-major-national-security-threat/.

"Majority Say January 6th Was an Attack on Democracy, Quinnipiac University National Poll Finds: About a Quarter of U.S. Still Not Planning to Get Vaccinated." *Quinnipiac Poll*. May 27, 2021. Retrieved from https://poll.qu.edu/images/polling/us/us05272021_ussb63.pdf.

Morton, Ella. "The *X-Files* 'I Want to Believe' Poster's Origin Story." *The New Republic*. Dec. 29, 2015. Retrieved from https://newrepublic.com/article/126715/x-files-i-want-believe-posters-origin-story.

Saad, Lydia. "Do Americans Believe in UFOs?" *Gallup*. Aug. 20, 2021. Retrieved from https://news.gallup.com/poll/350096/americans-believe-ufos.aspx.

Saad, Lydia. "Larger Minority in U.S. Says Some UFOs Are Alien Spacecraft." *Gallup*. Aug. 20, 2021. Retrieved from https://news.gallup.com/poll/353420/larger-minority-says-ufos-alien-spacecraft.aspx.

Notes

1. Saad, "Do Americans Believe in UFOs?"
2. "Majority Say January 6th Was an Attack on Democracy," *Quinnipiac Poll.*
3. Bowman, "Public Opinion on Conspiracy Theories."
4. Kennedy and Lau, "Most Americans Believe in Intelligent Life Beyond Earth; Few See UFOs as a Major National Security Threat."
5. Saad, "Larger Minority in U.S. Says Some UFOs Are Alien Spacecraft."
6. Morton, "The *X-Files* 'I Want to Believe' Poster's Origin Story."

1
UFOs or UAPs?

By Bzuk, via Wikimedia.

Skeptics often attribute UFO sightings to experimental military aircraft, and the saucer-shaped Avrocar single-man aircraft—pictured above during a 1961 test run—was developed as part of a secret US military project during the early years of the Cold War.

The US Military and UFOs in Fact and Fiction

When it comes to UFOs, it's difficult to separate fantasy from reality. UFO and alien stories have, over the past century, become one of the most familiar genres in fiction. Many Americans, and people around the world, have difficulty differentiating between the shared mythology of aliens and the actual, factual process of detecting and studying UFOs and related phenomena. A common feature to many kinds of UFO and alien stories is the involvement of military organizations. Because a nation's military is in charge of detecting and addressing any potential threat coming from land, air, sea, or even space, it is logical to imagine that the military would play a major role in any situation involving alien visitation. How the military is depicted in UFO fiction says a lot about how Americans envision their government, the nation's military, and the government's role in science.

One of the most common scenarios in UFO fiction involves hostile aliens involved in some sort of invasion and imagines how the United States or global military would respond. In films like *Independence Day* (1996) the US military is seen as heading a global effort to combat an immense alien threat. In other films and books, the US military might be depicted as playing a darker and often more malevolent role. Films like *E.T.* (1982) and *Super 8* (2011) depict the US military as involved in secret operations to capture and contain extraterrestrials from crashed UFOs. The military is depicted as an alarmist organization engaged in potentially unethical and immoral activities in the name of national security. This twist on the genre uses alien visitation to discuss xenophobia and to critique the standard military response to the unknown. Secretive military agencies are often depicted as being so focused on duty that they are willing to abduct and even kill humans to keep their secrets and to protect humanity from forbidden knowledge.

The fact that the US military serves as both villains and heroes in UFO stories reflects the complex relationship between the American people and their military. While a majority of Americans continue to express trust in the US military, trust has declined significantly in recent years. Polls in 2015 and 2018 found that around 70 percent of Americans trusted the military to guarantee their security and to represent American values in the broader world. Polls in 2020 and 2021 indicated that trust in the military has fallen to around 56 percent.[1] While Americans remain broadly patriotic about their military in times of crisis, there is a widespread perception that the military is also engaged in secretive activities of which the American people are only partially aware. This helps to determine whether Americans trust their military and what members of the military have to say in the realm of alien visitation as well.

How does the fantasy about military involvement with UFOs match up to the realities of military activity in the field of UFO science? Since the 1990s, polls have shown that a majority of Americans believe that the US government knows more about aliens than has been revealed to the public,[2] but is this actually the case? New developments between 2019 and 2021 brought Americans closer than ever to answering this question.

Credible Sightings?

America entered the 2020s in the midst of a massive surge of interest in UFOs. Much of this occurred because of key leaks of military videos and documents, followed by the voluntary release of previously classified information from the US Air Force and US Navy providing what some believed was among the most convincing evidence of alien visitation ever captured. The fact that military agencies and service members were among those recording these sightings seemed to give credence to the claim that some UFO sightings might be actual alien vessels or probes.

An unusual confluence of factors helped to provide momentum to the growing UFO craze, including the fact that the COVID-19 pandemic saw more and more Americans spending time at home and engaging in new hobbies and activities, like searching the skies (or the internet) for information about alien life and extraterrestrial visitors. As people around the world confined themselves to their homes, light and air pollution briefly but dramatically declined, and this contributed to a massive increase in UFO sightings in 2020, in comparison to the year before. While some believe that the increase in UFO sightings might mean an increase in actual alien visitation, a more plausible explanation is that a decrease in light pollution from vehicles, coupled with more recreational time in the home at night and the increase in media coverage meant that more people were looking up at the skies and had more opportunities to see unexplained things up there.[3]

In June of 2021, the US government released a major intelligence report providing details of US military and governmental sightings of UFOs and new information about the way that the government has managed UFO research. First off, in military and government reports, unidentified flying objects are better known as "unidentified aerial phenomena," or "UAPs," which helps to differentiate these official sightings and reports from the more generalized public interest and reported encounters with UFOs.

To the great disappointment of many UFO aficionados, the June 2021 report on UFOs by the Department of Defense did not confirm the existence of aliens or reveal any new government evidence that would support that hypothesis. However, the report did indicate that there have been many sightings of UAPs for which there is currently no functional explanation. In other words, the report stated that there is no evidence of alien technology discovered in any of the encounters with UAPs past or present, but it also stated that the United States cannot rule out the possibility that some of the unexplained UAP sightings might represent alien technology.[4]

The DoD report stated specifically that there are at least 143 UAP sightings that cannot currently be explained. In some of these encounters, the objects detected appear to accelerate in ways that seem impossible given current technology. In other cases, UAPs have been spotted engaging in changes of direction and submerging in water in ways that defy efforts to provide credible technological explanations. In total 18 incidents appeared to show UAPs that had no visible means of propulsion that were able to move against the wind, to remain stationary despite wind currents, or to maneuver in the wind in ways that could not be explained given current knowledge of aerial technology. While there is no evidence to suggest extraterrestrial origin, these 18 sightings are the most suggestive component of the report, indicating the existence of some unknown type of flight technology.[5]

Outside of the faint possibility of extraterrestrial visitation, some security, military, and tech experts have suggested that unexplained UAP sightings might indicate that some private company, inventor, or some other nation has developed new and innovative flight technology that has yet to be revealed to the public. Such technology, if it exists, could pose a significant security problem for the United States, and this is one of the reasons that UAP sightings have been kept secret.[6] The DoD report indicates that there was no evidence to suggest that the UAP sightings listed represented secret US technology, but this does not rule out the possibility that some other nation or private organization has developed drones or other flight technology capable of performing feats that cannot currently be explained.

As of 2019, the newly created Space Force, actually a reorganization of institutions that already existed under Air Force supervision, is the military branch most directly involved in UAP investigation, but the role that this emerging military organization will play remains unclear. One of the reasons that UAP sightings have been kept secret is to prevent service members who have been involved in sightings from being marginalized or judged because of these unusual encounters. Space Force has likewise been reluctant to openly describe the organization's plans for addressing UAP issues because the organization is still trying to define its role, and officials in the Space Force hope to establish credibility in the public view, rather than becoming associated with fringe science and interests.

The perception that UAP sightings represent a potential threat again raises questions about the military's role in investigating space and aerial phenomenon. One of the things that the June 2021 DoD report revealed was that the military has tended to avoid sharing data with civilian scientists as part of the broader effort to keep military data, especially potentially sensitive data, confidential. However, the report also indicates that military specialists and experts have been unable to gather enough data to explain at least 143 UAP sightings. This means that the military does not have the expertise or data to make any further determination on these mysteries and yet has also failed to fully utilize expertise from the civilian realm.

UFO investigator Robert Sheaffer said, after studying the 2021 government report, "Some people think that the government know more about UFOs, or UAP, than the public, but it's clear that they know less on the subject than our best civilian UFO investigators, not more."[7]

Another recent film in the alien visitation genre, *The Arrival* (2016), provided an interesting commentary on the role of the military in explorations of the unknown. In the film, global military organizations take control of the effort to address the arrival of a number of ships carrying multiarmed aliens. The US military, as is their role, treats the alien visitors as a potential threat, though calmer minds prevail and the military calls upon scientists to help them determine how to respond. A failure in communication frightens military representatives, and the military nearly launches an all-out attack on the alien ships until a scientist and language expert is able to better translate the aliens' language and reveals their benevolent intentions.

UAP sightings seem, to some, like a potential threat, but they are also representative of the many aspects of the universe of which humanity still has little knowledge or understanding. Finding satisfying answers to these questions is not likely a task that the world's military industrial complex can achieve, because the true expertise needed to investigate the world's mysteries depends civilian scientists and experts who dedicate their lives to explicating these mysteries.

Works Used

Barnes, Julian, and Helene Cooper. "U.S. Finds No Evidence of Alien Technology in Flying Objects, but Can't Rule It Out, Either." *New York Times*. Sept. 1, 2021. Retrieved from https://www.nytimes.com/2021/06/03/us/politics/ufos-sighting-alien-spacecraft-pentagon.html.

Cillizza, Chris. "8 Takeaways from the Government's Big UFO Report." *CNN*. June 28, 2021. Retrieved from https://www.cnn.com/2021/06/27/politics/ufos-uap-extraterrestrial-life/index.html.

David, Leonard. "Experts Weigh in on Pentagon UFO Report." *Scientific American*. June 8, 2021. Retrieved from https://www.scientificamerican.com/article/experts-weigh-in-on-pentagon-ufo-report/.

Nir, Sarah Maslin, "With More Time to Look Up, Sightings of UFOs Surged in the Pandemic: 'People Are Reporting These Events.'" *The Baltimore Sun*. Apr. 9, 2021. Retrieved from https://www.baltimoresun.com/news/nation-world/ct-aud-nw-nyt-ufo-sightings-20210409-ztqchqcgzrcflbfedk3c7wjkk4-story.html.

Saad, Lydia. "Americans Skeptical of UFOs but Say Government Knows More." *Gallup Poll*. Sept. 6, 2019. Retrieved from https://news.gallup.com/poll/266441/americans-skeptical-ufos-say-government-knows.aspx.

Shane, Leo III. "Trust in the Military Is Dropping Significantly, New Survey Suggests." *Military Times*. Mar. 10, 2021. Retrieved from https://www.militarytimes.com/news/pentagon-congress/2021/03/10/trust-in-the-military-is-dropping-significantly-new-survey-suggests/.

"UFO Report: US Finds No Explanation for Sightings." *BBC News*. June 25, 2021. Retrieved from https://www.bbc.com/news/world-us-canada-57619755.

Notes

1. Shane, "Trust in the Military Is Dropping Significantly New Survey Suggests."
2. Saad, "Americans Skeptical of UFOs but Say Government Knows More."
3. Nir, "With More Time to Look Up, Sightings of UFOs Surged in the Pandemic: 'People Are Reporting These Events.'"

4. Barnes and Cooper, "U.S. Finds No Evidence of Alien Technology in Flying Objects, but Can't Rule It Out, Either."
5. Cillizza, "8 Takeaways from the Government's Big UFO Report."
6. "UFO Report: US Finds No Explanation for Sightings," *BBC*.
7. David, "Experts Weigh in on Pentagon UFO Report."

"'They Want People to Take Them Seriously': Space Force Wary of Taking Over UFO Mission"

By Bryan Bender
Politico, August 8, 2021

The Pentagon is considering giving the Space Force a greater role in a stepped-up effort to track and investigate reports of UFOs. But the newest military branch isn't over the moon about the idea.

Space Force leaders are still struggling to rebrand an organization that has been lampooned since before its birth. Now, they are conflicted about becoming the military's go-to on what the Pentagon now calls "unidentified aerial phenomena," according to five current and former officials taking part in the discussions.

Advocates for the Space Force taking over for the Navy, which is currently leading the Pentagon's task force responsible for studying them, believe the new service is better suited to oversee a more robust effort aimed at collecting information on UFOs, and that its association with a topic of such public fascination, particularly among young people, could even boost recruiting.

"It makes perfect sense," said one former intelligence official who is advising the military in the planning, citing its more expansive geographic responsibilities than other military branches and access to global—and even galactic—surveillance technologies through the U.S. Space Command. "There is no limit to the Space Force mission. It doesn't have a geographic boundary like the other services."

But the former official also said some fear it will only deepen the branch's public relations challenge by providing more material for the jokes, science-fiction-themed memes and other forms of popular ridicule that the Space Force has endured since it was championed by then-President Donald Trump in 2018, who made it an applause line in his political rallies.

"They really are sensitive to that," the former official said. "They want people to take them seriously. They don't want to do anything that is embarrassing. But this is national security. This is their job."

The deliberations over what to do next about the unexplained sightings of high-performance aircraft are part of a new push to establish a more permanent government research effort.

A June report to Congress from the director of national intelligence concluded

---

that all but one of 144 UFO sightings that were reviewed could not be explained, including 18 that appeared to exhibit advanced properties.

The unclassified summary stated that "we currently lack sufficient information in our dataset to attribute incidents to specific explanations." It also concluded that the unknown craft "clearly pose a safety of flight issue and may pose a challenge to U.S. national security."

In response, the undersecretary of defense for intelligence and security is developing a plan to "formalize the mission" after being instructed by Deputy Defense Secretary Kathleen Hicks.

In a memo to senior military leaders following the report's release, Hicks sought a plan "for the establishment and operation of the new activity, to include the organizational alignment, resources and staffing required, as well as any necessary authorities."

The issue has primarily been overseen by a temporary Pentagon UAP Task Force that was stood up in 2020 and led by the Navy, whose pilots, radars and other surveillance systems have compiled most of the recent reports of unexplained sightings.

The Pentagon has provided few details about the deliberations over what will replace the task force. "Planning for an activity to take over the UAPTF's mission is ongoing," said Pentagon spokesperson Susan Gough.

The Space Force declined to address the internal deliberations. The Department of the Air Force, which oversees the Space Force, also deferred questions to Gough.

Congress, which requested the UAP report, is also planning to play more of a role.

The Senate's version of the fiscal 2022 Intelligence Act includes several provisions on the subject, including requiring classified reports to Congress on UAP sightings and analysis every quarter, as well as calling on all agencies to share any data they have so that a more comprehensive UFO file can be compiled for further study.

A congressional staffer also told *Politico* the classified portion of the bill includes a provision outlining more parameters for tackling the subject over the longer term, including recommending additional funding to finance the effort.

A former Pentagon official also said he expects there will also be legislative guidance on UAPs in a final version of the National Defense Authorization Act.

But in addition to the Space Force, which works in tandem with the newly reestablished U.S. Space Command, officials are considering a number of military and intelligence organizations at this early stage that could take the lead or combine their efforts in a new organization.

One is the secretive Space Security and Defense Program, which reports to both the Pentagon and the director of national intelligence, which oversees all spy agencies.

The outfit has a broad writ to assess potential space threats and also has authority to award contracts to develop new collection capabilities. Other candidates for a greater role in overseeing UFO issues are the Defense Intelligence Agency, which studies foreign weapons systems and has a history of researching such sightings, as well as the North American Aerospace Defense Command in Colorado, which is responsible for defending the nation's airspace.

> **There is no limit to the Space Force mission. It doesn't have a geographic boundary like the other services.**

Chris Mellon, a former senior Pentagon intelligence official and congressional staffer who has been advising the military on the topic, said whoever is tasked with leading a more permanent effort needs to be willing to work closely with numerous military, intelligence and law enforcement agencies across the government as well as the academic and scientific communities and the public.

"NORAD would seem to make sense, but again its willingness to share information with other organizations is questionable. Still, they have money and contracting authority and the heft needed to make changes to the status quo if they were willing to aggressively pursue the issue," he wrote in a recent blog post.

"Regardless," he added, "the first and most important step for Congress to take is to either identify a permanent home for the mission or require DoD and the [intelligence community] to do so and to explain their resulting rationale with the oversight committees."

Print Citations

CMS: Bender, Bryan. "'They Want People to Take Them Seriously': Space Force Wary of Taking Over UFO Mission." In *The Reference Shelf: UFOs,* edited by Micah L. Issitt, 9-11. Amenia, NY: Grey House Publishing, 2022.

MLA: Bender, Bryan. "'They Want People to Take Them Seriously': Space Force Wary of Taking Over UFO Mission." *The Reference Shelf: UFOs,* edited by Micah L. Issitt, Grey House Publishing, 2022, pp. 9-11. House

APA: Bender, B. (2022). "They want people to take them seriously": Space Force wary of taking over UFO mission. In Micah L. Issitt (Ed.), *The reference shelf: UFOs* (pp. 9-11). Amenia, NY: Grey House Publishing.

Why the Military Should Work with Scientists to Study the UFO Phenomenon

By Chris Impey
Military Times, July 15, 2021

UFOs have been in the news a lot lately. I am a research astronomer who has written and edited books and created a free online course about the search for life in the universe. While I think we are making progress on detecting life beyond Earth, I view UFOs from a skeptical standpoint, since the evidence that they represent aliens visiting the Earth is unconvincing.

Last month, a report from the Office of the Director on National Intelligence dropped on Congress. It described 144 sightings by military personnel over a 17-year period, preferring to use the term UAP, for unidentified aerial phenomenon, in part to avoid the stigma attached to UFOs.

For those like me waiting for definitive statements, the report was a big disappointment. It declined to draw any conclusions, saying the available data is "largely inconclusive" and noting it is limited and inconsistently reported. The report worried about increased air "clutter," and left open the possibility that some UAP sightings represent advanced technologies of foreign adversaries, with significant national security implications.

As for UFOs as alien spacecraft, the report was agnostic. It scrupulously avoided using the words alien or extraterrestrial. That will do little to discourage "true believers." Nearly half of all Americans think aliens are visiting the Earth, and the UFO phenomenon has become enmeshed in a web of conspiracy theories that include accounts of abduction by aliens and crop circles. These conspiracy theories have undoubtedly been fueled in part by the fact that the military has been secretly investigating UFOs for decades. Any rational debate over UFOs must contend with the fact that they have taken deep root in the public consciousness.

Will the report, and increased transparency by the military, change anything? Will it help draw scientists like me into a serious study of the phenomenon?

Scientists will have to get over their reticence to engage with the sightings. We are in an awkward position. Rapid progress in finding planets orbiting other stars has led to a projection of 300 million habitable planets in our galaxy. There has been plenty of time for life on some of those planets to evolve intelligence and technology. We don't deny the possibility of aliens traveling from their star system to ours. We are just unconvinced by the data presented so far. Most sightings can be attributed to weather balloons or astronomical phenomena such as meteors, fireballs, and Venus. There are many resources giving mundane explanations for UFO sightings.

There have been academic studies of UFOs before. In 1968, the Condon Report said that that no scientific knowledge had been gained from two decades of study of the phenomenon. But 20 years later, a review led by Stanford professor Peter Sturrock concluded that some sightings are accompanied by physical evidence that warrants investigation. It is telling that after decades of studies and hundreds of thousands of sightings, UFOs have not reached the gold standard in science for confirming any hypothesis: reproducible evidence.

For their part, the military and intelligence communities will have to more actively engage with scientists, and ask for their help and expertise in understanding the sightings in the report, and many others that have not been made public. There are signs that this might happen. Under Avril Haynes, the Office of the DNI has been drawing on its expert group of 500 scientists who consult with the intelligence agencies on scientific problems. A model for this type of collaboration is the two panels of scientists and medical experts that were recently set up to understand the "Havana syndrome" that has afflicted American diplomats since 2016.

What would a collaboration with scientists look like, and what kind of data would it take to "move the needle" on understanding the UAP phenomenon?

The recent report shows how difficult it is to interpret the sightings, even with expert observers and data from multiple sensors. In all but one of 144 cases, there was too little information to even broadly characterize the event. Deputy Defense Secretary Kathleen Hicks acknowledged this deficiency when she called for more timely and consistent data collection on UAPs. The Defense Department has just over two months to develop a new strategy and report back to Congress.

> **Sensors malfunction and even expert observers can be fooled when seeing something outside their realm of experience.**

Sensors malfunction and even expert observers can be fooled when seeing something outside their realm of experience. With optical and infrared imaging, it is extremely difficult to gauge the distance, size, and speed of an object. For example, the three Navy videos that have been in heavy circulation on the Internet seem impressive and inexplicable, but they could easily be artifacts of camera optics and tracking systems.

The military should invite a select group of experts to examine all the evidence (with suitable clearance given when the sensor technology involved is classified). It should be an interdisciplinary team, comprised to address all the observational characteristics of the phenomena. Ideally, data should be shared among our allies, since UAP appear globally. Scientists can bring their assets to bear on the problem as well. For example, civilian satellites are being used to detect and monitor UAPs and machine learning can be used to sift the data for anomalous events.

Scientists are curious and they love a challenging problem. I would lend my hand to the effort if asked. Let's hope the government will harness scientific expertise to shine light on this decades-long mystery.

Print Citations

CMS: Impey, Chris. "Why the Military Should Work with Scientists to Study the UFO Phenomenon." In *The Reference Shelf: UFOs,* edited by Micah L. Issitt, 12-14. Amenia, NY: Grey House Publishing, 2022.

MLA: Impey, Chris. "Why the Military Should Work with Scientists to Study the UFO Phenomenon." *The Reference Shelf: UFOs,* edited by Micah L. Issitt, Grey House Publishing, 2022, pp. 12-14.

APA: Impey, C. (2022). Why the military should work with scientists to study the UFO phenomenon. In Micah L. Issitt (Ed.), *The reference shelf: UFOs* (pp. 12-14). Amenia, NY: Grey House Publishing.

Those Amazing Navy UFO Videos May Have Down-to-Earth Explanations, Skeptics Contend

By Andrew Dyer

San Diego Tribune, May 29, 2021

UFO enthusiasts are having their moment ahead of the release of a congressionally mandated report on what the Pentagon calls "unidentified aerial phenomenon." The coverage of Navy videos purporting to show evidence of strange, unknown aircraft has featured the voices of so-called ufologists—UFO researchers—and Navy pilots who say they've seen mysterious objects in the skies off San Diego and the East Coast.

> *For the record:*
> *11:40 a.m. May 29, 2021 A previous version of this story incorrectly said former Navy pilot David Fravor filmed Navy UAP videos in 2015. Fravor was a witness to the 2004 sightings but did not film any of the videos.*

Crews on Navy warships have reported seeing unidentified aircraft similar to those captured on video. Other accounts detail mysterious drone sightings by the crews of Navy destroyers west of San Clemente Island. The island serves as a training base and ship to shore gun range for the Navy.

But as the videos revived decades-old theories of extraterrestrial visitation, the frenzy has been frustrating for those who specialize in debunking hoaxes and conspiracy theories. These skeptics point to more down-to-earth explanations.

"There's nothing new here, it's the same grainy videos we're used to seeing," said Michael Shermer, the founding publisher of *Skeptic* magazine.

In August, the Defense department established the Unidentified Aerial Phenomena Task Force after Sen. Marco Rubio, R-Fla., added language into the Defense Intelligence Authorization Act that called on the Pentagon to produce a report on unidentified aerial phenomenon within 180 days. When former President Donald Trump signed the massive government stimulus and appropriations bill on Dec. 27, the defense intelligence bill was included, and the clock started ticking.

The Pentagon will deliver its UAP report to Congress in June. The UAP Task Force's examination of unidentified phenomenon is ongoing, a Pentagon spokesman said last week.

Retired Navy Lt. Cmdr. Alex Dietrich, one of the Navy fighter pilots who said she saw an unidentified aircraft near San Diego in 2004, told the *Union-Tribune*'s Kristy Totten on her *News Fix* podcast recently she is wary of the UFO community's jumping to conclusions.

"Just because I'm saying that we saw this unusual thing in 2004 I am in no way implying that it was extraterrestrial or alien technology or anything like that," Dietrich said.

She also said she doesn't expect the Pentagon report to provide the kind of answers many are looking for.

"I think that the report's going to be a huge letdown," Dietrich said. "I don't think that it's going to reveal any fantastic new insight."

Navy Acknowledges Videos

Three of the most well-known videos were taken by Navy F/A-18s over both the Pacific and Atlantic. The three—known as "Gimbal," "Go Fast" and "Flir1"—were filmed by Navy Advanced Targeting Forward Looking Infrared, or ATFLIR, pods which attach to the fuselage of the aircraft.

Flir1, which was filmed off the coast of San Diego in 2004, was published anonymously on a UFO website in 2007, according to a 2020 *Popular Mechanics* report on the history of the video. In 2017, it received renewed attention when it was published by the *New York Times*. Flir1 and two additional videos were published by former Blink-182 guitarist Tom DeLonge's "To the Stars Academy of Arts and Science" website in 2019.

After the release of the videos, the Navy acknowledged they were real, calling the objects in the videos "unidentified aerial phenomenon."

In 2020, the Pentagon released the three videos itself. In a statement, it said it did so "in order to clear up any misconceptions by the public on whether or not the footage that has been circulating was real, or whether or not there is more to the videos." The Pentagon said at the time the phenomena observed in the videos remained characterized as "unidentified."

The Nimitz Encounter

Mick West, a former video-game designer, is one of the best-known skeptics pushing back on the claims of UFO enthusiasts. On his website, Metabunk.org, and on his YouTube channel, West experiments with cameras to show how light and motion can deceive viewers.

The three videos released by the Navy were filmed by infrared cameras. FLIR1 was captured off the coast of San Diego in 2004 by a fighter operating off the aircraft carrier *Nimitz*, while Go Fast and Gimbal were captured by an F/A-18 operating off the carrier *Theodore Roosevelt* off the coast of Florida in 2015.

West said that FLIR1 and Gimbal, and the images on them—described by some as showing aircraft with no directional control surfaces, intake or exhaust—are consistent with what could be expected if you filmed a fighter jet flying away from the camera. The apparent shapes of the aircraft — one saucer-like, the other like a Tic Tac—are due to glare on the lens of the camera, not proof of flying saucers, West maintains.

> **Another factor affecting people's perception of these videos, is the fact that the cameras themselves are moving at high rates of speed.**

"What we're seeing in the distance is essentially just the glare of a hot object," West said as he watched the FLIR1 video with the *Union-Tribune*. "So we're looking at a big glare, I think, of an engine—maybe a pair of engines with an F/A-18—something like that."

As for the maneuvers the craft appears to make, West said that the information on the screen, such as the zoom level, indicates that it's not the mystery aircraft making sweeping motions, but the camera. When the object appears to dart off to the left, that is actually an effect of the camera losing lock and moving to the right.

Another factor affecting people's perception of these videos, West said, is the fact that the cameras themselves are moving at high rates of speed. At the forward end of the ATFLIR pod is an electro-optic sensor unit that houses an internal gimbal assembly and an external rotating housing. In order to maintain a "lock" on an object, both the gimbal and the outer housing are in constant motion—as is the F/A-18 to which the pod is attached.

Combined with the high zoom rate of the camera, the resulting image might reflect a parallax effect—with the relationship of the object and its background changing depending on the angle of view, similar to how electrical poles appear to zoom past on the highway while more distant objects remain still.

Eyewitnesses to the FLIR1, or so-called *"Nimitz* encounters," tell a different story. The day before FLIR1 was shot, other F/A-18 pilots, including Dietrich, also saw a Tic Tac-shaped object in the air.

"We encountered this thing that we refer to as the Tic Tac because that's what it looked like," Dietrich said. "It was unlike anything we'd ever seen (and) unlike anything I've seen since. That's why we refer to it as 'unidentified.' We came back to the ship, we gave our reports and then went on with our training—went on with our lives and our careers."

Several sailors on board the San Diego-based guided missile cruiser *Princeton* say they also saw the objects in the 2004 encounter. Five former *Princeton* sailors told *Popular Mechanics* in 2019 that their ship's brand-new radar system began detecting unidentified aircraft performing extraordinary aeronautical maneuvers. They said the objects appeared on the radar to descend from 60,000 feet to just 50 feet in a matter of seconds.

It was these radar tracks that led to Dietrich and her wingman to divert and attempt to intercept the aircraft. The next day, another pilot was able to lock onto something with his ATFLIR—resulting in the video now known as FLIR1.

A Touch of Trig

The parallax effect also offers a more mundane explanation of the Go Fast video, West contends. Go Fast was shot from a Navy jet operating off the coast of Florida with the aircraft carrier *Theodore Roosevelt* in 2015. In the video, a small undefined object appears to be flying low, at a high rate of speed above the ocean.

However, West said, this is an illusion of the two-dimensional video, one that can be demystified by the readout on the screen and a little trigonometry.

Once the camera locks onto the object, West said, the video presents the illusion that the camera is stationary. This isn't the case, West said. The jet's true air speed is 369 knots. After factoring in the altitude of the aircraft, the angle of the camera and the distance to the target, West determined the object to be flying at 13,000 feet above the ocean—not directly above, as it appears in the video.

"It's not actually anywhere near the ocean even though it looks like it's skimming over the surface," West said. "Because of the extreme zoom and because the camera is locked onto this object ... the motion of the ocean in this video is actually exactly the same as the motion of the jet plane itself. You're seeing something that's actually hardly moving at all and all of the apparent motion is the parallax effect from the jet flying by."

After a little more math, West estimated the speed of the UAP to be about 30 to 40 knots. Since the infrared image indicates the object is also colder than the ocean below it, and it's moving at the wind speed of that altitude, West said he thinks it's likely a weather balloon.

"Complicated Illusion"

Perhaps the most striking of the three officially released Navy videos is Gimbal. Also filmed off the Florida coast in 2015, Gimbal appears to show a large object the shape of a top rotate in a manner inconsistent with known aircraft.

West admits that the object's rotation is difficult to explain. "Gimbal is complicated—you've got this ridiculous illusion of movement when it's actually essentially the same thing" as FLIR1, he said.

Still, West said the object in Gimbal is most likely just another jet.

"I think what's clear about Gimbal is it's very hot—it's consistent with two jet engines next to each other and the glare of these engines gets a lot bigger than the actual aircraft itself so it gets obscured by it," West said.

The odd top-like shape, West said, might be attributed to diffraction spikes from the glare, similar to someone taking a picture of a flashlight shining directly into a camera lens.

To explain the apparent rotation, West pointed again to the ATFLIR pod and the parallax effect. Early in the video, the F/A-18 is in a left bank turn, West said.

"At the start of the video, it looks like the object is moving rapidly to the left because of the parallax effect," he said. But when the plane has kind of finished its turn, it looks like it slows down and stops because now it's flying straight toward it so there's no parallax. You get this complicated illusion."

The rotation of the object, West said, can be attributed to the gimbal roll of the electro-optic sensor unit of the ATFLIR pod trying to maintain lock on it. He again points to the information on the display screen in the video.

"Gimbal starts off at 54 degrees left and it goes all the way to 7 degrees right," West said. "At 3 degrees left is when (the object) makes its big rotation. That is the point at which (the ATFLIR pod) is doing a large exterior correction for the gimbal roll."

The Gimbal and Go Fast videos were shot by the same pilot, according to former Navy pilot David Fravor. Fravor, one of the *Nimitz* pilots who saw the 2004 Tic Tac, told podcaster Lex Fridman in 2020 that he isn't moved by West's explanation.

"It's funny how people can extrapolate stuff who've never operated the system," Fravor said of West's critique. Fravor also told Fridman there were up to five other objects in the air that day flying in formation with the "Gimbal" aircraft and that several other sailors were tracking them.

A spokesperson for defense contractor Raytheon, which designed the ATFLIR cameras, declined to comment and referred questions to the Pentagon. The *Union-Tribune* also asked UC San Diego, California Institute of Technology, Massachusetts Institute of Technology and Embry-Riddle Aeronautical University to make experts on infrared camera and electro-optic technology available to comment for this story. None did.

The "Bokeh Effect"

Two videos taken on Navy surface ships were published this year by filmmaker Jeremy Corbell, who also runs the website ExtraordinaryBeliefs.com. Corbell's films explore phenomenon such as alien craft allegedly hidden from the public by the government and humans with alien implants.

One of the videos, which appears to be a sailor's cell-phone video of a night-vision screen, seems to show a triangular or pyramid shaped craft with flashing lights flying over the San Diego-based guided-missile destroyer *Russell* in 2019.

In the video, which is saturated in green night vision, one of the pyramid-shaped objects blinks periodically. Corbell told Fox News "this is probably the best UFO military filmed footage certainly that I've ever seen, but I think also that the world has ever seen."

West said the video is an example of a well-known photographic effect that occurs when a camera captures images of out-of-focus light called "bokeh."

In a video West shared on YouTube, he demonstrates how the effect works and essentially recreates what is seen in the Navy video.

West says any night-vision camera with a triangular-shaped aperture would show a green pyramid. The flashing of the object, West said, is identical to the navigation lights found on aircraft.

West further said that when one factors in the relative location of the ship and the date, that the other "pyramids" in the video are celestial objects—specifically the planet Jupiter and some stars. He points out the *Russell* was operating under the route aircraft take when flying from Hawaii to Los Angeles.

"There was just a whole bunch of planes flying overhead at the time," West said.

The most recent video appears to show a spherical blob flying above the ocean before diving into the wave or beyond the horizon. On Twitter, Corbell described the object as a "transmedium" vehicle, able to operate above and below the water. The video was filmed off the coast of California by the San Diego-based littoral combat ship *Omaha*.

West said the glare of an out-of-focus object with a heat signature might produce a similar image on an infrared camera. If that object is a jet aircraft flying away from the ship, West said, it might produce the same illusion of dropping into the water when, in fact, it had only flown over the horizon.

Known Unknowns?

While the military has confirmed the videos themselves are real, the Pentagon has not said whether it has since identified the objects—which West said gives the impression that the military either hasn't identified them or can't identify them.

The *Union-Tribune* asked the Defense department to clarify whether any of the unidentified phenomenon in the UAP videos have since been identified. Gough declined to do so.

"To maintain operations security and to avoid disclosing information that may be useful to potential adversaries, DOD does not discuss publicly the details of either the observations or the examination of reported incursions into our training ranges or designated airspace, including those incursions initially designated as UAP," Gough said.

Given that the objects have been seen in areas where the U.S. military trains, another hypothesis put forward is that the objects in the videos show advanced Chinese or Russian surveillance drones. Rubio, in his *60 Minutes* interview, pointed out the national security implications of that.

"Anything that enters an airspace that's not supposed to be there is a threat," Rubio said.

Dietrich told *News Fix* she's also concerned about adversaries.

"We want to know if there's something off our coast or in our skies," Dietrich said. "It could be a threat, it could be an adversary. We like to classify and categorize things and when we can't it's important to flag it."

For skeptics, even that possibility seems far-fetched.

Shermer, of *Skeptic* magazine, said that it's unlikely any government could develop technology that's significantly more advanced without detection by other "great powers."

"It would be like if we were still using rotary phones and they had smart phones—it would never happen," Shermer said. "Even with the Manhattan project, the most secret project ever, the Russians had the bomb four years later."

The Pentagon's refusal to debunk its own UFO videos is frustrating, Shermer said. And even if the June report is as mundane as Dietrich and others expect, he doesn't think it will matter to UFO enthusiasts.

"If the government issues a report saying it's all artifacts of camera, balloons, bokeh—the ufologists are not going to accept it," he said. "Nothing satisfies a true believer."

Print Citations

CMS: Dyer, Andrew. "Those Amazing Navy UFO Videos May Have Down-to-Earth Explanations, Skeptics Contend." In *The Reference Shelf: UFOs,* edited by Micah L. Issitt, 15-21. Amenia, NY: Grey House Publishing, 2022.

MLA: Dyer, Andrew. "Those Amazing Navy UFO Videos May Have Down-to-Earth Explanations, Skeptics Contend." *The Reference Shelf: UFOs,* edited by Micah L. Issitt, Grey House Publishing, 2022, pp. 15-21.

APA: Dyer, A. (2022). Those amazing Navy UFO videos may have down-to-earth explanations, skeptics contend. In Micah L. Issitt (Ed.), *The reference shelf: UFOs* (pp. 15-21). Amenia, NY: Grey House Publishing.

Pentagon Report Says UFOs Can't Be Explained, and This Admission Is a Big Deal

By Adam Dodd

The Conversation, June 27, 2021

A report from the US task force dedicated to investigating UFOs—or, in the official jargon, UAPs (Unidentified Aerial Phenomena)—has neither confirmed nor rejected the idea such sightings could indicate alien visits to Earth.

On Friday June 25, the Office of the Director of National Intelligence (ODNI) released its eagerly awaited unclassified intelligence report, titled *Preliminary Assessment: Unidentified Aerial Phenomena*.

The document is a brief nine-page version of a larger classified report provided to the Congressional Services and Armed Services Committees. It assesses "the threat posed by unidentified aerial phenomena (UAP) and the progress the Department of Defence Unidentified Aerial Phenomena Task Force has made in understanding this threat".

The report certainly does not, as many were hoping, conclude UFOs are alien spacecraft. Rather, it shows the task force hasn't made much progress since first being set up ten months ago. Perhaps this is unsurprising, given its task.

However, the task force's very existence would have been unthinkable to many people just one year ago. It's unprecedented to see the broader policy shift towards the acknowledgement of UFOs as real, anomalous physical phenomena that are worthy of extended scientific and military analysis.

Seemingly Advanced Technologies

The report withholds specific details of its data sample, which consists of 144 UFO reports made mostly by military aviators between 2004 and 2021. Its bombshell finding is that "a handful of UAP appear to demonstrate advanced technology".

This "handful"—21 of the 144 reports—represents classic UFO enigmas. These objects:

> appeared to remain stationary in winds aloft, move against the wind, manoeuvre abruptly, or move at considerable speed, without discernible means of propulsion. In a small

number of cases, military aircraft systems processed radio frequency (RF) energy associated with UAP sightings.

Its bombshell finding is that "a handful of UAP appear to demonstrate advanced technology."

These characteristics indicate some UAP may be intelligently controlled (because they aren't blown around by the wind) and electromagnetic (as they emit radio frequencies).

In March, Former Director of National Intelligence John Ratcliffe told Fox News some reports describe objects "travelling at speeds that exceed the sound barrier without a sonic boom". Sonic booms are sound waves generated by objects breaking the sound barrier.

No *known* aircraft can travel faster than sound without creating a sonic boom. NASA is currently developing "quiet supersonic technology", which may allow planes to break the sound barrier while issuing a subdued "sonic thump".

Some have claimed the objects are probably secret, advanced Russian or Chinese aircraft. However, global aerospace development has failed to match the flight characteristics of objects reported since the late 1940s. And it seems counterproductive to repeatedly fly secret aircraft into an adversary's airspace where they can be documented.

How Did We Get Here?

The report's release is a profoundly important moment in the history of the UFO mystery, largely because of its institutional context. To fully appreciate what this moment might mean for the future of UFO studies, we have to understand how the UFO problem has been historically "institutionalised".

In 1966, the US Air Force was facing increasing public pressure to resolve the UFO problem. Its effort to do so, then known as Project Blue Book, had become an organisational burden and a public relations problem.

It funded a two-year scientific study of UFOs based at the University of Colorado, headed by prominent physicist Edward Condon. The findings, published in 1969 as the *Final Report on the Scientific Study of Unidentified Flying Objects*, allowed the Air Force to end its UFO investigations.

Condon concluded nothing had come from the study of UFOs in the past 21 years that added to scientific knowledge. He also said "further extensive study of UFOs probably cannot be justified in the expectation that science will be advanced thereby".

Nature, one of the world's most reputable scientific journals, described the Condon Report as a "sledgehammer for nuts". But by then the Air Force had collected 12,618 reports as part of Project Blue Book, of which 701 sightings were categorised as "unidentified".

Unlike the new Pentagon report, the Condon Report didn't find any UFOs that appeared to demonstrate advanced technology. The most problematic cases were resolved by being categorised ambiguously. Here's one example:

> This unusual sighting should therefore be assigned to the category of some almost certainly natural phenomenon which is so rare that it apparently has never been reported before or since.

With this strategic category in the toolkit, there was no need to acknowledge seemingly advanced technology exhibited by UAPs. Indeed, they were deliberately filtered from institutional knowledge.

Recovering from "Institutional Forgetting"

For most of their postwar history, UFO reports have been regarded by state institutions as knowledge out of place, or "information pollution"—something to be excluded, ignored or forgotten.

The Pentagon's UAP task force represents an abrupt reversal of this longstanding organisational policy. UFO reports, made primarily by military personnel, are no longer pollutants. They are now important data with national security implications.

That said, they do still represent "uncomfortable knowledge". As the late Oxford University anthropologist Steve Rayner observed, knowledge can be "uncomfortable" for institutions in two ways.

First, Rayner said, "acknowledging potential information by admitting it to the realm of what is 'known' may undermine the organisational principles of a society or organisation".

Meanwhile, he said "not admitting such information may also have serious deleterious effects on institutions, either directly or by making them prone to criticism from other parts of society that they 'ought' to have known". Both aspects describe the institutional context of UFO information.

The US Department of Defence has confirmed UFOs threaten flight safety, and potentially, national security. In doing so, it has exposed a weakness in its organisational principles. It has admitted it's not very good at knowing what UFOs are.

It also faces the criticism that seven decades after UFOs first appeared on the radar, it *ought* to know what they are. The new Pentagon report doesn't compel us to accept the reality of alien visitation. But it does compel us to take UFOs seriously.

Print Citations

CMS: Dodd, Adam. "Pentagon Report Says UFOs Can't Be Explained, and This Admission Is a Big Deal." In *The Reference Shelf: UFOs,* edited by Micah L. Issitt, 22-25. Amenia, NY: Grey House Publishing, 2022.

MLA: Dodd, Adam. "Pentagon Report Says UFOs Can't Be Explained, and This Admission Is a Big Deal." *The Reference Shelf: UFOs,* edited by Micah L. Issitt, Grey House Publishing, 2022, pp. 22-25.

APA: Dodd, A. (2022). Pentagon report says UFOs can't be explained, and this admission is a big deal. In Micah L. Issitt (Ed.), *The reference shelf: UFOs* (pp. 22-25). Amenia, NY: Grey House Publishing.

The Upcoming Pentagon UFO Report Isn't the Place to Look for the Truth

By Eric Mack
CNET, June 24, 2021

The truth is out there, but it's almost certainly not going to be in the upcoming US Pentagon report to Congress on American military encounters with unidentified aerial phenomena, or UAP. They're the phenomenon previously referred to as UFOs. The landmark report is expected by Friday, June 25.

In case you've missed the latest chapter of the decades-long flying saucers space opera, some 21st century footage and eyewitness accounts from US Navy pilots support stories of objects making seemingly physics-defying maneuvers in the air (and into the ocean, in at least one case). The Navy has confirmed the veracity of the footage, much media attention has been dedicated to the topic and now a mandatory report to Congress from intelligence agencies on "advanced aerial threats" is due by June 25.

Early indications suggest the report will confirm that UAP are real, but that there's no reason to blame aliens or any other extraterrestrial influences for the weird things pilots and other military types are seeing.

For about three-quarters of a century now, since at least 1947 and the infamous Roswell crash, there has been significant suspicion that the government is withholding secret intelligence about UFOs. (The incident actually involved a government coverup of a program to detect Soviet atomic tests, not aliens.)

So is the long-awaited revelation of all the government knows finally at hand? Maybe. Probably not. But even if yes, it's bound to be a letdown.

The Truth Is in the Data

If UAP truly are mysterious and unidentified (there's at least one reason to doubt this key adjective truly applies; more on that later) in the eyes of the military, I would argue that the intelligence establishment is the wrong institution to solve the mystery.

While agencies like the CIA, the National Reconnaissance Office and the National Security Agency, especially when taken together with the rest of the intelligence establishment, are often perceived as all-seeing, all-hearing and all-knowing, they are also necessarily opaque, secretive and obviously protective of all the intelligence they gather.

And when it comes to solving what is essentially a scientific mystery like unidentified aerial phenomena, open collaboration based on transparency and the free flow of data and observations is what we really need.

I was thinking about this last week while reporting on the discovery of the most energetic gamma ray burst ever observed. GRBs are thought to be among the most powerful explosions in the universe, brought on by the collapse of a star. What's relevant here to the UAP discussion is the response to the initial detection of this super GRB. After it was detected by NASA satellites, an automatic notification went out to a network of observatories, and some were able to almost immediately begin gathering their own data.

The result of this open, instantaneous collaborative process was heaps of data that scientists were able to analyze, potentially leading to a new understanding of GRBs.

But when it comes to UAP, we have only grainy footage from radar and other cockpit instruments and maybe some other corroborating accounts from within the US Navy. This data has leaked out in dribs and drabs over years, long after the incidents took place. It's like trying to solve a murder that isn't even reported until years later, when the crime scene and the trail of clues have gone ice cold.

"It's impossible to say without access to the raw data and the people who claimed to see these things," Jonathan McDowell, a Harvard astrophysicist and humanity's unofficial archivist of all space launches, told me via email. "My position is that unidentified is not the same as unidentifiable, there's just not enough useful info to make an analysis."

McDowell says the lack of data makes him skeptical the now widely covered videos show any technology at all, alien or otherwise, "as opposed to birds, insects with the distance wildly mis-estimated, the planet Venus with the distance wildly wrong in the other direction, or sensor malfunctions for those not seen directly by a pilot's eyes."

There are, however, plenty who see something of interest in the videos without having to squint too hard, including a number of former intelligence heads, Sen. Harry Reid and former President Barack Obama, who have said the mystery is legit.

"We can't explain how they move, their trajectory," Obama said on the *Late Late Show* with James Corden. "They did not have an easily explainable pattern. And so I think that people still take seriously, trying to investigate [UAP] and figure out what that is."

Abraham Loeb, a controversial astronomer and author, has made waves in his quest to convince the world that the weird object called Oumuamua that cruised by Earth in 2017 was actually an alien spacecraft. He's made no such pronouncement about UAP, but he says it's notable these military sightings were detected by multiple instruments, including radar and infrared and optical cameras.

"It is possible, and likely, that most of the past reports on UFOs from the general public can be explained by human-made or natural phenomena or as illusions,

but we need to pay spe-
cial attention to the small
number of reports where
the evidence is strong and
undisputable."

But Loeb agrees with
McDowell that the key is
to collect more evidence.
Much more evidence.

Eyewitness accounts from US Navy pilots support stories of objects making seemingly physics-defying maneuvers in the air (and into the ocean, in at least one case).

"It would be prudent to progress forward with our finest instruments, rather than examine past reports," Loeb says. "Instead of declassifying documents that reflect decades-old technologies used by witnesses with no scientific expertise, it would be far better to deploy state-of-the-art recording devices, such as cameras installed on wide-field telescopes or audio sensors, at the sites where the reports came from, and search for unusual signals."

Loeb would like to see some sort of scientific initiative that attempts to repro-duce old reports of UFOs and UAPs in order to unravel their mysteries. He also says he'd be happy to lead such an inquiry and report back to Congress.

"This could take the form of a federally designated committee or a privately funded expedition. Its most important purpose would be to inject scientific rigor and credibility into the discussion."

Mystery or Manipulation?

All of this presumes that UAPs truly are a mystery to the US military, and here again we have to consider the secrecy that's ingrained within military and intelligence institutions. The Roswell incident has been attributed to a secret military recon-naissance project, and a number of UFO sightings can be traced to B-2 stealth bombers and other military aircraft that were once classified.

In 2016 the US Navy and an inventor named Salvatore Cezar Pais applied for a patent for a "craft using an inertial mass reduction device," which the US Patent and Trademark Office categorized as an "unconventional spacecraft propulsion sys-tem."

The patent, which was granted in 2018, describes a means of generating elec-tromagnetic fields that basically manipulate gravity in localized ways to create a vacuum around a spacecraft, reducing the effects of not only the craft's own mass, but also eliminating water and air resistance.

"As a result, extreme craft speeds can be achieved," the patent application reads. It also at one point mentions that "these systems would be strategically placed on an intergalactic craft."

The patent, along with a few others granted to Pais and the Navy, basically de-scribe the technologies that could enable the sorts of insane, physics-defying ma-neuvers that have been reported as UAP and will be included in the report to Con-gress later this month.

However, early indications are that the Navy, or some other secret military technology development program, is not about to take credit for being the actual source of any UAP in the report.

And it's important to note that filing patents for some far-out propulsion concepts doesn't necessarily mean that such technologies have actually been built or tested, or would even work as described.

But thanks to some document digging by the website *The Drive* in 2019, we know that the Navy had to convince the USPTO to grant the patent for Pais' futuristic craft after it was initially rejected on the grounds that it was either impossible or would require the energy of an entire star to work.

The Navy responded with a letter from Naval Aviation Enterprise Chief Technology Officer James Sheehy, explaining that, in fact, Pais was already testing some of the concepts involved. Sheehy then ends the note with some rather bold proclamations and revelations: "I would assert this will become a reality. China is already investing significantly in this area and I would prefer we hold the patent as opposed to paying forever more to use this revolutionary technology."

That's a lot to digest. To recap, Navy pilots and others in the military have reported UAP with incredible maneuverability over at least the past two decades. Footage of these encounters became public around the same time the Navy was applying for patents for craft capable of incredible maneuverability. The Navy has confirmed the veracity of UAP, but is expected to reveal in the forthcoming report that there's little reason to believe either alien or secret military technology is the cause of UAP.

Mmm-hmm.

One last interesting tidbit. *The Drive* notes that the Navy could have kept Pais' patents secret, but opted not to check the box to do so. It's enough to make you wonder whether the Navy wants someone or something—like the government of China, perhaps—to think that it might have such otherworldly capabilities. Are UAP just part of some geopolitical military mind games?

The US Naval Air Systems Command didn't immediately respond to a request for comment for this story.

It seems unlikely that the Navy and intelligence agencies or the scientific community will be providing any definitive answers on the origins of UAP in the coming weeks. But the search for the truth continues.

A new nonprofit dubbed UAPx is taking a scientific approach, using technology like satellites and artificial intelligence to monitor the area off the California coast where UAP have been sighted in the past.

And recently NASA administrator Bill Nelson told CNN that the agency is also beginning to investigate what's behind UAP.

"The bottom line is, we want to know," Nelson said.

Knowing may not be the same as believing, but I think Fox Mulder would still be happy to hear those words come from the head of NASA.

We'll see if we know more sometime between now and June 25. Stay tuned, and don't take your eyes off the skies for too long.

Print Citations

CMS: Mack, Eric. "The Upcoming Pentagon UFO Report Isn't the Place to Look for the Truth." In *The Reference Shelf: UFOs,* edited by Micah L. Issitt, 26-30. Amenia, NY: Grey House Publishing, 2022.

MLA: Mack, Eric. "The Upcoming Pentagon UFO Report Isn't the Place to Look for the Truth." *The Reference Shelf: UFOs,* edited by Micah L. Issitt, Grey House Publishing, 2022, pp. 26-30.

APA: Mack, E. (2022). The upcoming Pentagon UFO report isn't the place to look for the truth. In Micah L. Issitt (Ed.), *The reference shelf: UFOs* (pp. 26-30). Amenia, NY: Grey House Publishing.

2

Ancient Aliens and Modern Myths

Image courtesy of the Getty's Open Content Program, via Wikimedia.

An 1842 calotype of the moon by astronomer John Herschel, whose studies were falsely reported by the *New York Sun* in what became known as the "Great Moon Hoax."

The History of Aliens in American Culture

In 1835, readers of the *New York Sun* encountered a strange series of articles about the telescopic studies of Sir John Herschel, an English astronomer who had traveled to Africa to study the stars of the southern hemisphere. Herschel was at the forefront of astronomy and his expedition to South Africa resulted in the most accurate and detailed depictions of the lunar surface to date, but the actual products of this research, a barren rocky landscape pocked by craters but otherwise containing little variation and no signs of life, did not meet with what many believed would be the case when humans finally glimpsed the surfaces of the alien worlds long watched traversing the skies. Many stories of speculative fiction already imagined that the moon and the other planets might have vast civilizations and would be populated by intelligent beings. After all, seeing the tremendous diversity of life on earth, it seemed only logical to assume that the other planets would be likewise populated by living creatures.

Rather than publishing the actual results of Herschel's experimental study of the moon, the *New York Sun* hired Richard Adams Locke to write what was essentially a science fiction story about what Herschel found in his studies. Locke told readers that Herschel had constructed a telescope that was twenty-four feet in diameter and weighed in at seven tons. With this fantastic machine, he had "…solved or corrected nearly every leading problem in mathematical astronomy." In subsequent articles, Locke wrote that Herschel had seen white sand beaches and tall pyramids on the surface of the moon. Massive herds of bison-like creatures roamed desolate plains and there was also, the author stated in another article, a population of winged humanoids that the author called "man bats," or "Vespertilio-homo."[1]

The "Great Moon Hoax," as it came to be called, demonstrates that Americans had, for generations, been dreaming about the fantastic fictional worlds that might exist out among the stars, and stories that seemed to confirm this belief were embraced enthusiastically even if they seemed implausible. American UFO and alien mythology is likewise based largely on unreliable data and speculation more than on evidence, but the popularity of UFO mythology has not dissipated because it represents what many Americans would like to believe.

Aliens in Antiquity

Long before there were myths and legends about green or gray aliens visiting Earth in saucer-shaped craft or abducting humans for research, humans were already curious about the possibility of life outside the boundaries of the Earth. The earliest known example of what would later be called "science fiction" was written in 200 CE by the Turkish satirist Lucian of Samosata. Samosata's book *Very Historia*, or "True Story," talks about a journey to the moon, where the hero discovers three-headed vultures, birds constructed from leaves and pieces of flowers and plants, and insects as large as elephants. This was one of the first times that historic writers imagined what alien life might look like, though each of the creatures depicted by Samosata was simply a strange version of some lifeform found on Earth.[2]

Similar stories appear in early literature from Asia and Europe as well. Greek philosophers theorized about life beyond the solar system, though their imaginings reflected their polytheistic beliefs as much as any more scientific predictions about life on other worlds. Likewise, the famed Japanese story the "Tale of Princess Kaguya," or the "Bamboo Cutter," which was set on the moon, utilized Japanese Shinto myth to speculate on what life might be like on another world.

It wasn't until Charles Darwin's theory of evolution by natural selection was popularized in the West that images of alien life began to reflect the idea that organisms might evolve to fit their environments, rather than simply being fantastic versions of life found on Earth. One example can be found in the 1864 book *Real and Imaginary Worlds*, in which French astronomer Camille Flammarion described strange creatures, such as a version of humanity with backward facing toes on their heels and a single ear on top of their heads, that he saw as arising from the natural forces on another planet. It was a far cry from the much more scientific notions of alien life that came later, but it represented the beginning of what would later become "exobiology," the application of scientific principles to the study of extraterrestrial life.[3]

There are scattered works of science fiction stories from the early 1900s through the 1930s describing alien visitors coming to Earth, but there is no indication that Americans thought of UFOs as anything more than fiction until the late 1940s. It was during this period, post–World War II and with the Cold War looming, that a confluence of factors resulted in a surge of public interest in UFOs and aliens, and it was this period that created the characteristic mythology and imagery that is still associated with UFOs and alien visitation in American popular culture.

Becoming a National Craze

In 1947, pilot Kenneth Arnold was flying near Mount Rainier in Washington when he saw a glimmering object in the sky. He later claimed to have seen a series of strangely shaped objects flying in what looked like a purposeful formation. Arnold said that the objects looked like a saucer skipping across the water, and the newspapers described what Arnold had seen as "flying saucers." Media coverage of Arnold's sighting spread across the country. A Gallup poll in 1947 indicated that over 90 percent of Americans had heard about the incident in the month that followed the publication of the first reports.[4]

Arnold's sighting, which became known as the "Roswell incident" because it occurred near the town of Roswell, New Mexico, was explained later as the remains of a weather balloon, and most Americans lost interest after a short-lived boom in UFO mania. But, since 1947, there have been some Americans who continue to believe that Arnold actually saw alien craft in the desert that day in June and that the government hid that information from the public. From 1947 to the modern day, Roswell has played host to annual tourist boom from UFO and alien enthusiasts.[5]

While the military was dismissive of Arnold's claim in 1947, it was secretly concerned that the strange sightings of unexplained objects might mean that the Soviets or some other government had developed experimental aircraft that they were using for surveillance. The Pentagon organized a program to study UFO sightings, Project Blue Book, and between 1952 and 1969 government analysts representing the Central Intelligence Agency (CIA) and the military investigated more than 12,600 reported UFO sightings.[6]

As well concealed as the government's research into the issue might have been, stories of CIA and military agents visiting individuals who claimed to have spotted UFOs spread anecdotally through the United States, and this fueled the belief that the government knew more than it was letting on about UFOs. Another contributing factor was that the US government was, at the time, conducting secret aircraft experiments of its own, some of which happened in a facility in the desert of Nevada that came to be known, in the lore of alien enthusiasts, as "Area 51." While there were undoubtedly experimental aircraft being developed and tested at the Nevada site in the 1950s and 1960s, UFO enthusiasts claimed that the Air Force base in the area was where the military concealed the remains of alien wreckage and potentially even the bodies of aliens. As interest in Area 51 increased, the government's denials, even as the site was clearly being used for confidential technological research, only deepened the belief that the government was hiding UFO information in the Nevada desert.

One of the incidents investigated as part of Project Blue Book was an alleged case of alien abduction that occurred in 1961 in New Hampshire. The story of this abduction became the subject of dozens of articles, several full-length books, and even a film starring James Earl Jones. From this point on, alien abduction myths became an important part of American UFO legends, and this period also saw ideas about the physicality of aliens cohere into a common view of extraterrestrials as short green or gray creatures with enlarged heads and dark, almond-shaped eyes. This now ubiquitous image of alien life became so familiar that smartphones even include the green-headed alien image as an emoji. The period from the introduction of the alien craze after Roswell to the alien abduction trend of the 1960s and 1970s shaped the stereotypical view of alien visitation, but none of the incidents and anecdotal sightings provided any evidence to substantiate claims that UFO visitation was real.

The Modern View

Over the years since the UFO craze of the 1960s, there have been a number of high-profile incidents involving alleged UFO sightings. In 1997, for instance, hundreds of residents in Phoenix, Arizona, spotted what many described as a large v-shaped flying object moving over a mountain range. Film of the strange event was posted to YouTube and featured in numerous television news reports, and press coverage of the incident went nationwide. Local military authorities provided explanations for the phenomenon that included dropping military flares, but many refused to accept this explanation and maintained that the Air Force claims were part of a cover-up masking a legitimate alien encounter.[7] In 2010, seven former members of the US Air Force told stories of either first-hand encounters or second-hand stories of unidentified objects appearing above nuclear missile silos. UFO researcher Robert Hastings said in press coverage of the incident that he believed aliens were trying to send a warning to Americans and Russians about nuclear proliferation.[8]

The 1997 "Phoenix lights" sighting was one of the first captured with quality video equipment, and so was one of the first such events in which Americans were able to scrutinize the image on their own. Many Americans found the film convincing, so much so that they refused to believe Air Force explanations that did not involve extraterrestrial visitors. In the years since, a variety of captivating information has been presented on UFO sightings, including the release of newly declassified videos showing Navy and Air Force personnel encountering unidentified objects that appear to fly in ways considered impossible given modern flight technology.

While there have been many compelling UFO sightings over the decades, the one thing that is still missing is solid, physical evidence of alien visitation. Compelling personal anecdotes and images clear enough to demonstrate something unusual are interesting but cannot be taken as proof that aliens have visited the Earth. Physical evidence is needed of technology of nonhuman origin or of alien visitation. Until such evidence is found, it is likely that most Americans will remain skeptical and that passionate belief in UFOs and alien visits to the Earth will remain primarily a fringe interest in which mainstream audiences play but do not commit.

Works Used

Hendley, Matthew. "The 'Phoenix Lights' Are No Mystery." *New Times*. Mar. 14, 2014. Retrieved from https://www.phoenixnewtimes.com/news/the-phoenix-lights-are-no-mystery-6661825.

Lagrange, Pierre. "A Ghost in the Machine: How Sociology Tries to Explain (Away) American Flying Saucers and European Ghost Rockets, 1946-1947." *Imagining Outer Space*. 2012. Retrieved from https://link.springer.com/chapter/10.1057%2F9780230361362_12.

Nerlich, Brigitte. "Camille Flammarion: Making Science Popular." *University of Nottingham*. July 22, 2016. Retrieved from https://blogs.nottingham.ac.uk/makingsciencepublic/2016/07/22/camille-flammarion/.

"Project BLUE BOOK–Unidentified Flying Objects." *National Archives*. 2021. Retrieved from https://www.archives.gov/research/military/air-force/ufos.

Scharf, Caleb A. "The First Alien." *Scientific American*. Nov. 23, 2019. Retrieved from https://blogs.scientificamerican.com/life-unbounded/the-first-alien/.

Scoles, Sarah. "How UFO Sightings Became an American Obsession." *Wired*. Mar. 3, 2020. Retrieved from https://www.wired.com/story/how-ufo-sightings-became-an-american-obsession/.

"UFOs Eyed Nukes, Ex-Air Force Personnel Say." *CNN*. Sept. 27, 2010. Retrieved from https://news.blogs.cnn.com/2010/09/27/ufos-showed-interest-in-nukes-ex-air-force-personnel-say/.

Zielinski, Sarah. "The Great Moon Hoax Was Simply a Sign of Its Time."

Smithsonian. July 2, 2015. Retrieved from https://www.smithsonianmag.com/smithsonian-institution/great-moon-hoax-was-simply-sign-its-time-180955761/.

Notes

1. Zielinski, "The Great Moon Hoax Was Simply a Sign of Its Time."
2. Scharf, "The First Alien."
3. Nerlich, "Camille Flammarion: Making Science Popular."
4. Scoles, "How UFO Sightings Became an American Obsession."
5. Lagrange, "A Ghost in the Machine: How Sociology Tries to Explain (Away) American Flying Saucers and European Ghost Rockets, 1946-1947."
6. "Project BLUE BOOK–Unidentified Flying Objects," *National Archives*.
7. Hendley, "The 'Phoenix Lights' Are No Mystery."
8. "UFOs Eyed Nukes, Ex-Air Force Personnel Say," *CNN*.

From Flying Boats to Secret Soviet Weapons to Alien Visitors—A Brief Cultural History of UFOs

By Greg Eghigian

The Conversation, July 8, 2021

When Did the Idea of UFOs First Emerge?

The idea of aliens and that other worlds might be inhabited actually goes back to ancient times. The question was a matter of real debate among philosophers, scientists and theologians in the Western world by the 18th century and it was widely accepted that alien civilizations existed.

But something changed in the 19th century. That's when you first start to see these reports of people seeing what they say were flying ships overhead. The things people describe back then sound a lot like the things they were familiar with–they literally saw ships and vessels that would normally float on the sea in flight. Some people would see steam-powered ships.

But it's really not until the summer of 1947 that people began to regularly speak of seeing flying objects that some attributed to extraterrestrials.

What Happened in 1947?

A pilot by the name of Kenneth Arnold was flying his small plane near Mount Rainier in Washington state. As he was flying around he said he saw some sort of glimmer or shine that caught his eye and was concerned that maybe he was going to have a collision with another aircraft. When he looked, he saw what he described as nine very odd-shaped vessels flying in formation.

After Arnold landed, he reported his sightings to authorities at a nearby airport and eventually talked to some reporters. When a reporter asked Arnold to describe how the things moved, he said, "they flew like a saucer would if you skipped it across water." Some very clever enterprising journalists came up with the headline "flying saucers" and from that point forward they were flying saucers–even though Arnold never uttered the phrase himself.

A Gallup poll six weeks after the event discovered that 90% of Americans had heard the term flying saucer. This was the beginning of the phenomenon that some call the flying saucer era and the contemporary idea of UFOs.

Within days other people in the country began reporting having

> **A considerable number of UFO sightings were people seeing secret airplanes like the U2.**

seen similar things in the sky. Within weeks the U.S. Air Force decided to look into the reports. Arnold's story also triggered a lot of press interest and soon the international media were covering this story. It was a worldwide phenomenon within months.

Who Starts to Look into UFOs?

Two things happened in parallel: First were government-sponsored investigations in the U.S., specifically within the Air Force. Starting in 1947 the Air Force set in motion a number of different projects all basically interested in one question: Do UFOs represent a national security threat? The government wasn't interested in a deep scientific analysis of these things.

On the other hand, from 1947 to 1950 you had a lot of the general public who were just utterly fascinated with the mystery of flying saucers. What are they? Are they real? If they are real, who's behind them? Some people threw around the idea of aliens, but that's not really the major theory that people bought into. Most people—if they thought the sightings were real—believed they were either secret weapons of the U.S. military or secret weapons or secret aircraft of the Soviets.

So out of this fascination developed what you could call the equivalent of fan groups—flying saucer clubs. Those became the seeds of growth in the 1950s and 1960s for UFO organizations first at the local, then the national and then the international level.

How Did Government Programs Fit into the UFO Ecosystem?

A lot of what the Air Force did was behind closed doors and supposed to be clandestine. The government has released files over many years that show that a considerable number of UFO sightings were people seeing secret airplanes like the U2. It's no surprise that the Air Force would try to keep strict control over what's revealed to the public.

But that strict control is one of the many things that fed conspiracy theories over the years. The idea among UFO believers became "The government isn't shooting straight with us. Somehow we've got to get these people to disclose all the information they know."

What Is the Modern American Perspective on UFOs?

Up until the '90s the Cold War played a really fundamental formative role in how people in the U.S. imagined UFOs—both in terms of how we think about humanity's prospects technologically, but also relating to the fears and anxieties surrounding the Cold War. But when the Cold War ended, interest fell off. From the late 1990s into the early 2000s media coverage was nominal.

That all changed with the 2017 revelations about the secret UFO project in the Pentagon. This spurred on a resurgence of interest in UFOs. The way the media were talking about UFOs had lot of the same elements from before: Are these things alien? If they're not alien, are they from our military or somebody else's military? Are the people who were pushing the narrative and stories of sightings operating in good faith or are these con men?

In so many ways this was all really reminiscent of the 1940s and 1950s.

Do You See a Shift in How Scientists Think of UFOs?

In my conversations with scientists I've been seeing some movement toward a willingness to say, "This stuff is maybe worthy of looking into more seriously." The important change since the 1990s–specifically for astrophysicists and astronomers–has been the discovery of so many planets around other stars that could possibly support life.

I'm excited by the prospect of deeper study–both as a phenomenon that needs to be investigated by physical scientists but also as a social and cultural phenomenon. Mystery breeds speculation, and the UFO phenomenon is not a puzzle that can be easily solved. The mystery part gives people an opportunity to ask big questions about not just humanity's place in the universe, but about the limits of technology and knowledge. I think that's why people keep returning to the question of UFOs.

Print Citations

CMS: Eghigian, Greg. "From Flying Boats to Secret Soviet Weapons to Alien Visitors—A Brief Cultural History of UFOs." In *The Reference Shelf: UFOs,* edited by Micah L. Issitt, 39-41. Amenia, NY: Grey House Publishing, 2022.

MLA: Eghigian, Greg. "From Flying Boats to Secret Soviet Weapons to Alien Visitors—A Brief Cultural History of UFOs." *The Reference Shelf: UFOs,* edited by Micah L. Issitt, Grey House Publishing, 2022, pp. 39-41.

APA: Eghigian, G. (2022). From flying boats to secret Soviet weapons to alien visitors—A brief cultural history of UFOs. In Micah L. Issitt (Ed.), *The reference shelf: UFOs* (pp. 39-41). Amenia, NY: Grey House Publishing.

UFOs Were Born Among America's Cold War Fears

By Kate Dorsch
Foreign Policy, June 6, 2021

The U.S. Senate is currently awaiting an official report detailing everything the government knows about unidentified flying objects (UFOs) and unidentified aerial phenomena (UAPs). The report is the result of a provision in the $2.3 trillion 2020 appropriations bill that provided coronavirus relief to Americans and avoided a government shutdown. It is expected, among other things, to address the now infamous Advanced Aerospace Threat Identification Program (AATIP), made famous by reporting in late 2017.

The current UFO-mania centers on a series of sightings made by U.S. Navy pilots or appearing on their sensors in 2004, 2014, and 2015, the video and reports of which were leaked by former U.S. Defense Department official Luis Elizondo. Elizondo's alleged credibility derives from his claim to have served as director of AATIP. He described the program as "understandably overstretched" and without "the resources that the mounting evidence deserved." His effort to ignite interest in un- or underreported military sightings has been bolstered by the creation of To the Stars Academy of Arts and Science (TTSA), a research institute co-founded by UFO true believer and former Blink-182 frontman Tom DeLonge, and former CIA official Jim Semivan. Elizondo now works with TTSA in the company of another former U.S. intelligence official, Christopher Mellon. The credentials of both the Navy pilots and the former government officials involved in TTSA have kept these sightings, and the controversy around them, in the public eye for more than three years.

Amid the breathless media reporting and calls for transparency, accountability, and the American people's "right to know," it is easy to get caught up in the excitement and mystery. Why are the Pentagon and the respective branches of the U.S. military investigating UFO/UAP sightings? Will we finally receive confirmation that aliens are real and visiting us? Or that we're being surveilled by some advanced aerial Big Brother technology? What is the government hiding from us?

Yet while Elizondo's 2017 leaks may have come as a revelation to some, the U.S. military complex has been investigating reports of strange aerial phenomena for almost 75 years. Understanding UFOs and UAPs as historically embedded in airborne global war and U.S. national security concerns explains why they are an object of investigation and inquiry, why those investigations continue, and why sightings and witnesses maintain a persistent power to keep the U.S. public engaged and questioning—as it has several times in the past.

U.S. military involvement with the "UFO question" (What are they? Where do they come from?) dates back to the summer of 1947 and the birth of the modern UFO. We can track the modern UFO or "flying saucer" to the pilot and UFO godfather Kenneth Arnold's ur-sighting in late June 1947. While assisting in a search for a missing military transport plane over the Cascade Mountains in Washington state, Arnold reported seeing nine discrete flying objects zipping about the mountain peaks. He described them as silvery or metallic, fast, and appearing to be intelligently controlled. Arnold made note of the weather, the time, and used objects in his cockpit to estimate size and speed. When he landed, he told his colleagues. Then he told the press.

Arnold's sighting was followed by a series of copycat sightings. The sightings were first localized in the Pacific Northwest but quickly spread across the continental United States and then around the world. The U.S. Air Force, then the U.S. Army Air Forces, took serious interest in the sightings, given the descriptions it was receiving—that these were aerial technology, metallic, intelligently controlled, and terrestrial.

That Arnold's sighting takes place and receives the attention it does is no mere fluke of history but rather a deeply contingent event that hinges on its postwar moment. The modern UFO brought together and embodied three specific characteristics of the tensions of 1947.

First, the flying saucers of 1947 represented the technoscientific developments of World War II taken to the extreme. The world wars, and the second in particular, had led to unprecedented developments and progress in the technology and science of warfare. Major breakthroughs were made in submarine technology, aerial

> **The U.S. defense complex's concerns with UFOs has always been one of national security.**

technology (manned and unmanned), cybernetic command-control technologies, computing technologies, medical technologies, surveillance and sensor technology, and weapons technology. The appearance of strange, and potentially deadly, objects in the skies was a resonant idea in the wake of the V2 rocket attacks on London and the unleashing of the atomic bomb. These flying disks, many believed, could just be the next step in bomber technology.

1947 was also a pivotal year in the development of the Cold War. Though once allies, the spring of 1947 saw the American-Soviet friendship collapse, articulated in the Truman Doctrine of March 1947, which presented communism as a threat to the American way of life and pressed the need to contain that threat geopolitically. Americans were faced with, as they saw it, a new and alien challenger.

The summer of 1947 also witnessed the creation of the Air Force as an independent branch of the U.S. military. The Allied forces had won World War II thanks in large part to U.S. military support, especially superior U.S. air power. As a result, the U.S. Army Air Forces understood itself as not only the critical element of the Allied victory over fascism but as the foremost offensive power and first line of defense in future wars, which would certainly be airborne.

he Army Air Forces leveraged its military successes and philosophy of aerial warfare to lobby for its existence as an independent branch of the U.S. military (successfully achieved in July 1947) and for the ongoing support of a substantial research budget, meant to contribute to the cutting-edge research and development required to keep the newly created U.S. Air Force the global leader in aerial offensive and defensive capabilities.

The next war, fought between the United States and the Soviet Union, would be airborne and its threat existential, thanks to the newfound power of atomic weapons and the advance of aerial martial technology.

Humanity had been seeing strange things in the sky since the beginning of recorded history, but these developments transformed the UFO into a national security threat—and gave it a catchy acronym to boot. In its earliest days, it was understood to be terrestrial in origin and most likely Soviet. It distressed Air Force command greatly that the Soviets would have a technology so far advanced beyond its own; not only would this present an existential threat to the American public, but it also indicated that the Air Force was no longer the global leader in air power. The Air Force set out to identify (and one day, it was hoped, capture) these unknown aircraft invading American skies.

Over the next two decades, the Air Force would operate a series of investigatory projects meant to respond to sighting reports and identify the potential dangers posed by these objects. When Project Blue Book, the longest and most well-known of these projects, concluded in 1969, the Air Force did not stop investigating sightings made by its personnel. It merely folded those investigations into normal intelligence procedures. It is safe to presume that investigations of credible sightings by its pilots and other staff continue to this day.

The U.S. defense complex's concern with UFOs has always been one of national security. Given the ongoing pace of development in aerial technologies—surveillance, weaponry, aircraft, and so on—it should be unsurprising that the 21st-century Navy, Air Force, Pentagon, and U.S. intelligence community continue to investigate reports of strange aerial phenomena made by their personnel.

Indeed, even the current centering of Navy pilots as highly reliable witnesses has a historical precedent. Many of the cases investigated in the Air Force's early projects came from pilots and other military personnel. And reports that came from pilots were treated with a heightened degree of seriousness: Pilots were men, professionals who were experts in their skillset, serious-minded, sober, calm, even-tempered, and not prone to hyperbole or fanciful storytelling. Pilots have historically been treated as among the most credible witnesses. That standard remains in place and supports the ongoing controversy today.

As the release of the new report approaches, the public should temper its expectations about the contents. Similar reports have been organized and released before. Judging by the past, the report will recount the number of cases over the years, their location and frequency, who made them, and what evidence exists. Where cases can be "solved" and the phenomena identified, we should expect detailed accounts; where insufficient data exists to make a positive or "highly likely" confirmation, we should expect to see these phenomena remain "unknown" or "unidentified." That is not an endorsement of any theory about their origins, alien or terrestrial—simply an acknowledgement of the lack of clear evidence.

And the American public should not expect to see a full, unredacted version. U.S. military investigations have always been matters of national security. Where objects or phenomena have been identified as belonging to foreign nations or adversaries, the defense establishment will keep these cases hidden from view.

Historians are fans of Nietzsche's principle of eternal recurrence—put more clearly by *True Detective*'s Rust Cohle: "Time is a flat circle. Everything we've ever done, or will do, we're going to do over and over and over again." The pattern of public excitement about UFOs certainly repeats itself. But regardless of what the upcoming report holds, the U.S. defense and intelligence complex has always understood UFOs and UAPs as a national security matter. In a world of aerial surveillance and drone warfare, this won't change anytime soon.

Print Citations

CMS: Dorsch, Kate. "UFOs Were Born Among America's Cold War Fears." In *The Reference Shelf: UFOs,* edited by Micah L. Issitt, 42-45. Amenia, NY: Grey House Publishing, 2022.

MLA: Dorsch, Kate. "UFOs Were Born Among America's Cold War Fears." *The Reference Shelf: UFOs,* edited by Micah L. Issitt, Grey House Publishing, 2022, pp. 42-45.

APA: Dorsch, K. (2022). UFOs were born among America's Cold War fears. In Micah L. Issitt (Ed.), *The reference shelf: UFOs* (pp. 42-45). Amenia, NY: Grey House Publishing.

In New Book, Retired Air Force Major Claims Alien Was Killed at Joint Base McGuire-Dix-Lakehurst

By Erik Larsen
Asbury Park Press, September 3, 2019

Was an alien shot and killed in the Pine Barrens of New Jersey?

A new book, titled *Strange Craft: The True Story of an Air Force Intelligence Officer's Life with UFOs*, claims that a military police officer shot an extraterrestrial being at Fort Dix in the early morning hours of Jan. 18, 1978.

In the book by author John L. Guerra and published by Bayshore Publishing Co. of Tampa, Florida, retired Air Force Major George Filer III—a decorated former intelligence officer for the 21st Air Force, Military Airlift Command at the adjacent McGuire Air Force Base—recounts the extraordinary tale from America's disco age.

Filer, now 84 and living in Medford with his wife, Janet, said what has been an urban legend first promulgated by UFO enthusiasts since the early 1980s is indeed true. That's because he was there and wrote a top-secret memo about it, he said.

Could it be a UFO?

In the freezing winter darkness of that day in January 1978, a bipedal creature, described as about 4 feet in height and grayish-brown in color, with a "fat head, long arms and slender body," was shot to death with five rounds fired from a service member's .45-caliber (military issue M1911A1) handgun.

As Guerra explains it in his book, the soldier had originally been in a police pickup truck, driving through the wilderness of the base in pursuit of a strange, low-flying aircraft that had been observed passing through the military installation's airspace about 2 a.m. that morning.

About an hour into the drive, the soldier became aware—in typical, horror movie fashion—that the craft, oval-shaped and radiating a blue-green glow, was hovering directly over his vehicle.

UFOs in New Jersey: What Has Been Spotted Above the Shore?

That's when the "creature" emerged from the shadows on foot, revealing itself to the soldier by stepping into the beams of the vehicle's headlights where

> The idea that the universe was filled with intelligent and civilized beings had been a staple of the popular culture since the start of the space race.

the panicked MP drew his weapon, ordered the alien to freeze, and he fired.

According to the retired major as told in the book, the alleged alien succumbed to its gunshot wounds on the Air Force side of what is now Joint Base McGuire-Dix-Lakehurst in Burlington County; its remains giving off a foul-smelling, ammonia-like stench.

Later that morning, a cleanup crew from Wright-Patterson Air Force Base in Ohio—headquarters of the National Air and Space Intelligence Center—flew in to retrieve the body, behaving as if the creature was, well, not entirely alien to them.

The *Asbury Park Press* reached out to the Air Force at the Joint Base for comment about this story, but never heard back.

Filer, who has most recently served as the state director for an organization called MUFON (the Mutual UFO Network, which catalogs and investigates UFO sightings throughout the United States), never actually saw the dead alien. However, Filer said he knows for a fact that the story is true. It should be noted that Filer has claimed to have seen UFOs throughout his entire life, starting when he was 5 outside his boyhood home in Illinois.

"There Are UFOs Buzzing Around the Pattern Like Mad"

On that January morning in 1978, Filer said he arrived on base before dawn to prepare his daily 8 a.m. intelligence briefing for his superior officers. In the book, he explains that when he arrived, security at the base had been tightened and he personally observed the emergency response in the aftermath of the incident. He also said he interviewed some of the witnesses from the scene for a report on what happened that he was required to file. However, he was denied access to and was never cleared to see photos that he said were taken at the scene.

"The senior master sergeant runs everything, from who sweeps the floors to organizing the staff schedules and making sure phones and faxes are up and running," Filer is quoted in the book. "He was agitated; his face was pale and his eyes were wide open. Then he said the strangest thing: 'An alien has been shot at Fort Dix and they found it on the end of our (McGuire AFB) runway.'"

Aliens in NJ?: 70 Years Ago at the Shore, UFOs Filled the Sky

Filer said he replied: "Was it an alien from another country?"

"No, it was from outer space, a space alien," the sergeant explained. "There are UFOs buzzing around the pattern like mad."

Later, the Air Force classified everything as top secret and silenced the witnesses through national security restrictions and good old-fashioned intimidation. Everyone that is, except Filer.

Filer has spoken publicly about the 1978 incident before and the incident itself has been the subject of discussion and speculation in the UFO enthusiast community since the early 1980s. Details about it appear to have been first reported in *The Trentonian* on July 10, 2007.

The Trentonian had reported 12 years ago that the Air Force repeatedly denied the claim, telling the newspaper that "the case was discredited as a hoax years ago."

UFOs Were All the Craze in the 1970s

It's perhaps important to understand the era in which the incident took place. Five years after the end of the Apollo moon program, the imagination of most Americans remained captivated by the seemingly endless possibilities of space travel.

The idea that the universe was filled with intelligent and civilized beings—perhaps hundreds or thousands of years more advanced than humans—had been a staple of the popular culture since the start of the space race between the United States and Soviet Union.

On Jan. 18, 1978, Steven Spielberg's blockbuster hit *Close Encounters of The Third Kind*—a movie about little gray aliens with fat heads, long arms and slender bodies visiting Earth amid a government cover-up—was still playing in local movie theaters two months after its release date.

Indeed, an ad for the film appears on page A6 in the *Press* from that date with the tagline "We Are Not Alone," over a brilliant light emanating from just over a mountainous horizon, down a long road.

During the previous summer of 1977, the original *Star Wars* had debuted and was not just a mega-blockbuster hit, but made terms such as "Darth Vader" and "The Force" part of the lexicon of the culture.

We've got all the news covered at the Shore, whether it's happening on the ground or in the sky. So consider a digital subscription to APP.com and support local journalism, it's out of this world.

UFO sightings carried an air of greater credibility back then—there were 377 references to UFOs published in the *Press* between 1977 and 1978, compared to 85 references between 2017 and 2018.

Even President Jimmy Carter had acknowledged that he had seen one, a decade earlier. He had made a post-Watergate campaign promise in 1976 to learn whatever secrets about UFOs the government may have been hiding.

Everyone was looking up for strange lights in the night sky back then, including NASA. The Associated Press reported just two days before the McGuire-Dix incident, that the federal space agency had outlined in a memo to the Carter White House that it was willing to analyze "bona fide evidence from credible sources."

Then there was the matter of the strange booms from the sky that were heard over the Jersey Shore and indeed much of the East Coast between December 1977 and March 1978, which had frightened some of the population.

The phenomena had started on Dec. 2, 1977 and was violent enough that it caused a tremor in southern Ocean County. Indeed, officials at the Oyster Creek nuclear power plant in Lacey had ordered the evacuation of non-essential staff on that day out of an abundance of caution.

The scientific consensus at the time was that the noise came from the supersonic Concorde, the British-French airliner—transatlantic service to John F. Kennedy International Airport in New York had begun a week earlier—that could travel twice as fast as the speed of sound. The sonic boom was thought to have been augmented by a combination of frigid atmospheric conditions and a slight deviation from the aircraft's normal flight path.

However, the data was inconclusive and subsequent booms did not necessarily conform to the Concorde's schedule.

In the past few years, there has been renewed interest in UFO phenomena after declassified video and audio last year showed U.S. Navy pilots apparently encountering a strange aircraft as they flew their Boeing F/A-18 Super Hornet fighter jet off the East Coast in 2015.

In June, President Donald Trump told *ABC News*' George Stephanopoulos that he had been briefed about the subject matter but expressed skepticism that extraterrestrial beings were operating some kind of vehicle within Earth's atmosphere.

"People are saying they're seeing UFOs. Do I believe it? Not particularly," Trump said.

Aliens or not, what if anything, happened at McGuire Air Force Base on Jan. 18, 1978? Whatever it was, it's now part of folklore of the Pinelands—and beyond.

Print Citations

CMS: Larsen, Erik. "In New Book, Retired Air Force Major Claims Alien Was Killed at Joint Base McGuire-Dix-Lakehurst." In *The Reference Shelf: UFOs,* edited by Micah L. Issitt, 46-49. Amenia, NY: Grey House Publishing, 2022.

MLA: Larsen, Erik. "In New Book, Retired Air Force Major Claims Alien Was Killed at Joint Base McGuire-Dix-Lakehurst." *The Reference Shelf: UFOs,* edited by Micah L. Issitt, Grey House Publishing, 2022, pp. 46-49.

APA: Larsen, E. (2022). In new book, retired Air Force major claims alien was killed at Joint Base McGuire-Dix-Lakehurst. In Micah L. Issitt (Ed.), *The reference shelf: UFOs* (pp. 46-49). Amenia, NY: Grey House Publishing.

Roswell UFO Crash: What Is the Truth Behind the "Flying Saucer" Incident?

By David Crookes
Space, May 5, 2021

There is a spaceship that looks like a flying saucer in Roswell. Thousands of motorists drive past it every day, and hundreds of people go inside. It's on North Main Street in this southeastern New Mexico city, its metal skin gleaming as it basks in the glow of the sun. Its neon lighting burns into the retinas of those who view it throughout the evening, and it's rather hard not to admire. After all, aside from its striking looks, who doesn't fancy a burger every now and then? That's right: This spacecraft is one of the city's McDonald's restaurants.

So why is the building shaped that way? It's not that far from the site of a mysterious incident which took place in 1947—the day when a rancher discovered debris scattered around his sheep pasture, prompting speculation that an unidentified flying object, or UFO, had crashed there.

In June, or possibly early July 1947, William Brazel had woken for a normal day's work on the J.B. Foster ranch in Lincoln County, New Mexico, 75 miles (120 kilometers) north of Roswell, when he made a shocking discovery. He found on the ranch "a large area of bright wreckage made up of rubber strips, tinfoil, a rather tough paper and sticks," Brazel said in an article published on July 8, 1947, in the *Roswell Daily Record*.

Brazel hadn't heard of flying saucers—at least not yet. Sightings, however, were coming in thick and fast around that time. On June 24, pilot Kenneth Arnold claimed to see nine unidentified objects "flying like a saucer would across water" near Mount Rainier, Washington. Arnold estimated that the objects were flying at around 1,200 miles per hour (1,930 kilometers per hour), Arnold was reported as saying in the *East Oregonian*, but at the time there were no known craft that could reach those speeds. The Air Force also said it had no new experimental planes or guided missiles that would fit such a description, according to a U.S. Department of Defense report. That story became front-page news, and the term "flying saucer was born, despite Arnold describing the flying objects as crescent-shape," according to *New Scientist*.

The country soon became gripped, as Brazel discovered. By July 7, policemen and astronomers were reportedly being harassed for further reports, this time by people from New York and other eastern states, and that was the day Brazel decided to take action. He hand-delivered a box of accumulated debris, which he'd gathered with the help of his wife and two children, to Sheriff George Wilcox of Roswell, according to *Smithsonian Magazine*.

By now there was talk of a reward for anyone who recovered one of these unidentified flying objects. In the *Roswell Daily Chronicle*, Brazel is stated to have "whispered kinda confidential-like" that his find may be one of the flying disks, so an equally intrigued Wilcox contacted Colonel William Blanchard, the commanding officer of the Roswell Army Air Field (RAAF), who sent agents to the site to gather the remaining material.

What happened next would cement the idea that the debris was the remnants of an alien spacecraft. According to David Clarke's book *The UFO Files: The Inside Story of Real-Life Sightings*, published by Bloomsbury in 2012, the RAAF's public information officer Walter Haut issued a press release on July 8: "The many rumors regarding

> **Failure to provide physical evidence means anecdotal accounts have spread misinformation.**

the flying disc became a reality yesterday when the intelligence office of the 509th Bomb Group of the Eighth Air Force, Roswell Army Air Field, was fortunate enough to gain possession of a disk through the cooperation of one of the local ranchers and the sheriff's office of Chaves County".

This was reported in the *Roswell Daily Record* along with the news that Major *Jesse A. Marcel* was the group intelligence officer dispatched to the scene. He'd gone with Counter Intelligence Corps officer Sheridan Cavitt, but on his way back took a detour to his own home, whipped out a couple of boxes of debris that he'd popped into the boot of his car and showed it to his 10-year-old son, Jesse Jr. One of the objects was said to have hieroglyphic-like markings, something that stuck in the mind of the young boy, according to a report in *The Guardian*.

But just as quickly as excitement of the find gathered pace, the Army took swift action in debunking the story. The very next day, shortly after government scientists began to arrive at the scene, it was claimed that the debris was actually from a crashed weather balloon, and Marcel was asked to be pictured at a press conference with the debris allegedly found. And that was that, case closed—or so everyone thought.

But interest began to grow again. In 1978, nuclear physicist, author and UFO researcher Stanton Friedman interviewed Marcel, who said that the discovery made 31 years earlier was not from this world, and that the government had ordered him to keep quiet. Friedman revisited the incident and sought other witnesses, and his work inspired Charles Berlitz and William Moore to write *The Roswell Incident*, published in 1980. Their conclusion was simple: there had been a huge cover-up.

The Flying Saucer Conspiracy Begins

Other things were happening in the world at the time. Notably, the sci-fi films *Star Wars* and *Close Encounters of the Third Kind* had just been released, and—as reported by *The Times*—studies since have suggested that sightings and belief in UFOs rise when popular films and TV shows make their debut. Nevertheless, testimonies about that day in 1947 were forthcoming, and they continued to come for many years.

Glenn Dennis called a hotline shortly after an episode of *Unsolved Mysteries* featuring the Roswell incident aired in 1989. He suggested that a friend who worked as a nurse at the Roswell Army Air Field saw three alien bodies, according to *Time Magazine*. But the real bombshell moment came in 1994. Could it be that the debris really was from an alien craft?

According to the U.S. Air Force, no. The weather balloon story was not true, but it wasn't to hide the fact that little green men had visited Earth. The wreckage was actually that of a classified project that flew microphones on high-altitude balloons so that sound waves generated by Soviet atomic bomb tests could be detected. Called Project Mogul, it was said to have run between 1947 and 1949. What's more, the balloons were claimed to have been made up of unusual material—the type that could easily be confused for a UFO. So, case closed? Not at all.

"The ever-changing accounts gave rise to uncertainty," Kenneth Drinkwater, senior lecturer in psychology at Manchester Metropolitan University, U.K., who specialises in the anomalous and paranormal, said via email. "The first message that went out was unclear. Then they changed the message, and it led to suspicion that something was going on and being covered up. It gives rise to a feeling that something is being hidden from the general population, leading to speculation of possible conspiracy and possibly alien technology."

It's why the Roswell files remain open in the eyes of many, and investigators put great value on the testimonies of those who were there, many of them respected military personnel. "Every member of Blanchard's senior staff, with a single exception, suggested the craft was of alien origin," Kevin D. Randle, a retired lieutenant colonel of the U.S. Army Reserve who served in Vietnam and Iraq, told *All About Space*. "Major Edwin Easley, the base provost marshal, told me, when asked if we were following the right path—meaning extraterrestrial—that it wasn't the wrong path."

The "single exception" is Cavitt, the retired lieutenant colonel of the Air Force who accompanied Marcel to the debris site. His careful testimony suggested that nothing untoward happened. He said he had never been threatened by anyone in government and that the debris wasn't extensively scattered. Yet UFO investigators say that if the wreckage was Project Mogul, then this testimony doesn't ring true. Mogul arrays were big, so the debris field would have been large.

"Everyone agrees that something fell at Roswell, but there is no terrestrial explanation," Randle told *All About Space*. "Project Mogul fails because the documentation tells us that flight number four—the alleged culprit—was cancelled. It did not fly. All other explanations have failed too: It wasn't an aircraft accident, not a rocket from White Sands and not a regular weather balloon."

Over the past 40 or so years there have been new claims and fresh leads, adding to the mystery and keeping the Roswell files very much alive. UFO investigator

Calvin Parker, for example, recently spoke of his time with Marcel before he died in 1986, claiming that Marcel revealed that he'd hidden three pieces of metal from the crash site in the top of his water heater in his house. They have never been recovered, however.

Many UFO investigators are keen to stress that they don't take every testimony at face value. Randle previously said that the credibility of Dennis must be discounted because of inconsistencies, and told *All About Space* that the accounts of military personnel are not simply accepted just because of their background. "There are some military witnesses who have been discredited as inserting themselves into the tale," Randle wrote via email. Likewise, there are civilian witnesses who are compelling.

"There are some very creditable civilian witnesses, such as Brazel and Frankie Rowe," said Randle. Rowe is certainly an interesting case. She was told of the crash by her father, a firefighter, who described creatures he had seen. According to Randle, Rowe said she was shown debris from the crash site, but had been told to stay quiet by the state. She says there was evidence her phone had been tapped. But of all of the witnesses, is too much weight being put on Marcel's account?

"If Marcel was standalone then there would be some real problems here, but he is not. There are many credible witnesses—men who achieved high military rank, men and women who were prominent in their communities—who believe the craft was alien," Randle said. "We have attempted to eliminate the fakers from those who had information to provide. We have been taken in, for a time, by some of those fakers, but in the long run it was we who investigated the case that removed many of those fakers, though based on evidence and not a belief there is no alien visitation. The point is that Marcel was backed up by other high-ranking officers, and many civilians who were part of the case. Marcel told what he had seen and done, and there was little embellishment in his testimony."

Randle appeared in the documentary, *Roswell: The First Witness*. It follows the investigations of former CIA operative Ben Smith into Roswell, and a key part of the series is a journal found in Marcel's possessions that was initially thought to have been written by him.

Speculation Continues: Was the Craft of Alien Origin?

It turned out that the journal—which consisted of quotes, lyrics and jokes—could be dated to the time of the Roswell incident, but the handwriting didn't match Marcel's. Smith pondered why the former army officer retained the journal, and there was speculation over whether it may have contained a code. If it did, however, it could not be deciphered by even the best of minds, according to the documentary.

Smith also sought to discover what was written in a document held by Brigadier General Roger Ramey, Eighth Air Force commander, during the press conference. It was captured in a photograph taken by *Star-Telegram* reporter J. Bond Johnson, and ufologists have long wondered whether the words they struggle to make out refer to "victims of the wreck." As Smith found, however, even the best technology could not sufficiently clean the document enough to make the words readable, and they remain a source of debate.

There were other interesting explorations in the documentary series. A body-language expert examined video interviews of Marcel and said it appeared that he was telling the truth, at least as he saw it. Experts including aviation crash investigator David Soucie were also taken to examine the crash site. Interestingly, the wind currents in the area were found to be inconsistent with a lightweight balloon crashing in the way that was described.

As the documentary continued, more evidence emerged. Crucially, there was a taped interview conversation between Marcel and author Linda G. Corley in which the military man discussed the items he found in 1947. "I found all this stuff and I was told to keep my mouth shut," he told her. "I held on to this premium for 32 years without saying anything at all. See, I was an intelligence officer. I handled intelligence and security for the base. I still hold an allegiance to my country, the vow that I took to keep my mouth shut about everything that might encroach on military secrets."

Just as compelling was an account from the family of Patrick Saunders, the 509th adjutant who is likely to have known about the whole event. He had apparently told people that it wasn't a weather balloon, but something similar to a jet fighter, that files were destroyed or changed and that the world wasn't ready for the truth because it would cause social upheaval. Were the "beings" friendly, he was said to have pondered.

This kind of testimony—particularly the first-hand testimony of Marcel that was chronicled in Corley's book, *For the Sake of My Country*—ensures the incident remains open. The fact the US government admitted there was a cover-up in 1994 only continues to add fuel to the fire.

Yet Drinkwater says failure to provide physical evidence means anecdotal accounts have spread misinformation, and he remains in doubt. "Colonel John B. Alexander offers an excellent insight into the myths and possible conspiracies connected to UFOs, the Roswell incident, the government involvement and so on," he said. "I think it's more about a sense of reality and how it can be swayed emotionally. I'm dubious about the nature of a secret operation where many might not have known about the goings on at their level."

So what of those who likely know: presidents past and present, perhaps? Former president Donald Trump told his son Don Jr. in an interview on YouTube in June 2020 that he'd heard some "interesting things" about aliens, thereby ensuring speculation will continue for some while yet.

"Would you ever open up Roswell and let us know what's really going on," Don Jr. asked, to which Trump responded: "There are millions and millions of people who want to go there and want to see it. I won't talk to you about what I know about it, but it's very interesting."

That's something countless people will no doubt chew over if they happen to visit and find themselves in that extraordinary McDonald's. Roswell is a town that will be forever linked to one of the greatest mysteries of all time, and we may never truly reach a consensus on the truth that is out there.

Print Citations

CMS: Crookes, David. "Roswell UFO Crash: What Is the Truth Behind the 'Flying Saucer' Incident?" In *The Reference Shelf: UFOs,* edited by Micah L. Issitt, 50-55. Amenia, NY: Grey House Publishing, 2022.

MLA: Crookes, David. "Roswell UFO Crash: What Is the Truth Behind the 'Flying Saucer' Incident?" *The Reference Shelf: UFOs,* edited by Micah L. Issitt, Grey House Publishing, 2022, pp. 50-55.

APA: Crookes, D. (2022). Roswell UFO crash: What is the truth behind the "flying saucer" incident? In Micah L. Issitt (Ed.), *The reference shelf: UFOs* (pp. 50-55). Amenia, NY: Grey House Publishing.

Army Officer's Secret Journal Could Offer New Clues About the UFO Crash in Roswell in 1947

By Mindy Weisberger
Live Science, December 11, 2020

A long-hidden diary belonging to a U.S. intelligence officer has rekindled research into the Roswell Incident, the infamous UFO crash in Roswell, New Mexico, that took place more than 70 years ago.

When a mysterious object slammed into the desert near the Roswell Army Air Field (RAAF) in July 1947, Maj. Jesse Marcel, an RAAF intelligence officer, was sent to supervise collection of the debris. A press officer at the RAAF issued a statement on July 8 describing "the crash and recovery of 'a flying disc,'" which many interpreted as evidence of alien contact. But the next day, another army official told reporters that RAAF officers had recovered a weather balloon, not a flying saucer.

Newspaper photos showed Marcel posing with pieces of what appeared to be a shredded high-altitude weather balloon with a radar reflector. But in the decades since, many have speculated about the military's initial "flying disc" report, wondering if the wreckage was perhaps more unusual than the photos implied. Recently, Marcel's family revealed that he had kept a diary from that period that might contain clues about the crash, sparking a new investigation by the History Channel in *Roswell: The First Witness*, part of the network's "History's Greatest Mysteries" series.

"The government claimed they had recovered a UFO—they had a press release about it," said Ben Smith, a former CIA operative and the show's lead investigator. "No other government in the world has said 'We have a spacecraft,' and then the next day there's another press release that says, 'Never mind, it was just a weather balloon'," Smith told *Live Science*.

The show revisits the Roswell crash site, incorporating aerial surveys and mapping, and using multispectral imaging to detect micro-depressions in the ground that could indicate where debris landed, Smith said.

But the central component of the new inquiry is a diary, which Marcel supposedly kept during the time of the Roswell crash, and which is now in the possession of his grandchildren. Decades after the event, Marcel told an interviewer that he believed the object that crashed in the New Mexico desert had extraterrestrial origins, *Time* reported in 1997. Analysis of the diary—and translation of its cryptic language—could reveal coded messages that Marcel wrote about the crash at the time that it happened, Smith said.

> **In 2017 and 2018, U.S. Navy pilots recorded three encounters with fast-moving UFOs.**

Interest in UFOs hasn't waned since the Roswell Incident—if anything, recent evidence has amplified it. In 2017 and 2018, U.S. Navy pilots recorded three encounters with fast-moving UFOs (also referred to as UAP, or unidentified aerial phenomena); the Navy officially declassified the videos in April of this year, *Live Science* previously reported. Also in 2017, a former Pentagon official confirmed the existence of a federal agency that had been secretly investigating UFOs since 2007, and which may still be active today.

But why do the events of Roswell still intrigue people?

"It's the origin story of the UFO, the prospect of a government cover-up for alien contact," Smith said. "Science fiction already existed but things that passed to us through pop culture found their origins in government secrecy surrounding this strange sequence of events in 1947," he said.

"It all starts in Roswell."

Print Citations

CMS: Weisberger, Mindy. "Army Officer's Secret Journal Could Offer New Clues About the UFO Crash in Roswell in 1947." In *The Reference Shelf: UFOs,* edited by Micah L. Issitt, 56-57. Amenia, NY: Grey House Publishing, 2022.

MLA: Weisberger, Mindy. "Army Officer's Secret Journal Could Offer New Clues About the UFO Crash in Roswell in 1947." *The Reference Shelf: UFOs,* edited by Micah L. Issitt, Grey House Publishing, 2022, pp. 56-57.

APA: Weisberger, M. (2022). Army officer's secret journal could offer new clues about the UFO crash in Roswell in 1947. In Micah L. Issitt (Ed.), *The reference shelf: UFOs* (pp. 56-57). Amenia, NY: Grey House Publishing.

Rancher Surprised at Excitement Over His Debris Discovery Near Roswell

By Trish Long
El Paso Times, June 27, 2017

In early July 1947, William Ware "Mack" Brazel reported finding debris on a ranch near Corona, N.M., about 80 miles northwest of Roswell. On July 8, the *Roswell Daily Record* reported that the intelligence office of the 509th Bombardment group at Roswell Army Air Field announced that they had come into possession of a flying saucer.

The story made worldwide headlines, but less than 24 hours later, the military changed its story.

In a July 9, 1947, Associated Press article, it was reported that the debris found by Brazel was actually from a weather balloon: An examination by the Army revealed Tuesday night that mysterious object found on a lonely New Mexico ranch was a harmless high-altitude weather balloon, not a grounded flying disc.

Excitement was high until Brig. Gen. Roger M. Ramey, commander of the Eighth Air Force with headquarters here, cleared up the mystery.

The bundle of tinfoil, broken wood beam and rubber remnants of a balloon were sent here Tuesday by Army Air Transport in the wake of reports that it was a flying disc.

But the general said the objects were the crushed remains of a wind target used to determine the direction and velocity of winds at high altitude.

Warrant Officer Irving Newton, forecaster at the Army Air Forces weather station here, said, "We use them because they go much higher than the eye can see."

The weather balloon was found several days ago near the center of New Mexico by rancher W.W. Brazel. He said he didn't think much about it until he went into Corona, N.M., last Saturday and heard the flying disc reports.

He returned to his ranch, 85 miles northwest of Roswell, and recovered the wreckage of the balloon, which he had placed under some brush.

Then Brazel hurried back to Roswell, where he reported his find to the Sheriff's Office.

The sheriff called the Roswell Air Field and Maj. Jesse A. Marcel, 509th bomb group intelligence officer, was assigned to the case.

Col. William H. Blanchard, commanding officer of the bomb group, reported the find to General Ramey and the object was flown immediately to the Army field here.

Ramey went on the air here Tuesday night to announce the New Mexico discovery was not a flying disc.

Newton said that when rigged up the instrument "looks like a six-pointed star, is silvery in appearance and rises in the air like a kite."

In Roswell, the discovery set off a flurry of excitement.

Sheriff George Wilcox's telephone lines were jammed. Three calls came from England, one of them from the London Daily Mail, he said.

A public relations officer here said the balloon was in his office "and it'll probably stay right there."

Newton, who made the examination, said some 80 weather stations in the U.S. were using that type of balloon and that it could have come from any of them.

He said he had sent up identical balloons during the invasion of Okinawa to determine ballistic information for heavy guns.

The following day an Associated Press article in the *Las Cruces Sun-News* said Brazel was sorry he said anything about his find:

"If I find anything else short of a bomb it's going to be hard to get me to talk," he told the Associated Press yesterday.

Brazel's discovery was reported Tuesday by Lt. Warren Haught, Roswell Army Air Field public relations officer, as definitely being one of the "flying discs" that have puzzled and worried citizens of 43 states during the past several weeks.

The statement was later discounted by Brig. Gen. Roger Ramey, commanding general of the Eighth Air Force of which the RAAF is a component. Ramsey said Brazel's discovery was a weather radar target.

The mysterious object found on a lonely New Mexico ranch was a harmless high-altitude weather balloon, not a grounded flying disc.

But Brazel wasn't making any claims. He said he didn't know what it was.

He described his find as consisting of large numbers of pieces of paper covered with a foil-like substance, and pieced together with small sticks, much like a kite. Scattered with the materials over an area about 200 yards across were pieces of gray rubber. All the pieces were small.

"At first I thought it was a kite, but we couldn't put it together like any kite I ever saw," he said. "It wasn't a kite."

Brazel related this story:

While riding the range on his ranch 30 miles southeast of Corona on June 14, he sighted some shiny objects. He picked up a piece of the stuff and took it to the ranch house seven miles away.

On July 4, he returned to the site with his wife and two of his children, Vernon, 8, and Bessie, 14. They gathered all the pieces they could find. The largest was about three feet across.

Brazel said he hadn't heard of the "flying discs" at the time, but several days later his brother-in-law, Hollis Wilson, told him of the disc reports and suggested it might be one.

"When I went to Roswell I told Sheriff George Wilcox about it," he continued. "I was a little bit ashamed to mention it, because I didn't know what it was.

"Asked the sheriff to keep kind of quiet," he added with a chuckle. "I thought folks would kid me about it."

Sheriff Wilcox referred the discovery to intelligence officers at the Roswell Army Air Field, and Maj. Jesse A. Marcel and a man in civilian clothes whom Brazel was unable to identify went to the ranch and brought the pieces of material to the air field.

"I didn't hear any more about it until things started popping," said Brazel. "Lord, how that story has traveled." Brazel said he did not see the thing before it fell, and it was badly torn up when he found it.

Print Citations

CMS: Long, Trish. "Rancher Surprised at Excitement Over His Debris Discovery Near Roswell." In *The Reference Shelf: UFOs,* edited by Micah L. Issitt, 58-60. Amenia, NY: Grey House Publishing, 2022.

MLA: Long, Trish. "Rancher Surprised at Excitement Over His Debris Discovery Near Roswell." *The Reference Shelf: UFOs,* edited by Micah L. Issitt, Grey House Publishing, 2022, pp. 58-60.

APA: Long, T. (2022). Rancher surprised at excitement over his debris discovery near Roswell. In Micah L. Issitt (Ed.), *The reference shelf: UFOs* (pp. 58-60). Amenia, NY: Grey House Publishing.

3
Secret Facilities

By X51, CC BY-SA 3.0, via Wikimedia.

A sign at the border of Area 51 warns that "photography is prohibited" and that "use of deadly force is authorized."

The Myths and Mysteries of Area 51

Since the 1950s, many have believed that evidence of alien technology was concealed in a top-secret military base in Southern Nevada, which became known as "Area 51." Interest in the alleged secrets contained within the base exploded in 2019 when an internet joke started a "movement" to "storm" the military facility and forcefully uncover the secrets allegedly kept there.

Birth of a Legend

The author Umberto Eco wrote in his novel *Foucault's Pendulum*, "A secret is powerful when it is empty. . . . As long as it remains empty it can be filled up with every possible notion, and it has power."[1] The legend of Area 51 serves as a prime example of Eco's premise—that secrets tend to have more appeal and allure before the truth is revealed. The rumors about Area 51 are widespread and varied. Some believe that the facility is used to house wreckage from alien spacecraft, while others believe that the bodies of actual aliens or even living aliens are contained within the facility. Some have even suggested that Area 51 contains a secret movie studio where the government filmed a "fake" moon landing in 1969. The primary reason that so many Americans have imbued the legend of Area 51 with so many fantastic claims is that the facility was, and remains, among the worst-kept secrets in American history.

In 2013, the Central Intelligence Agency (CIA), for the first time in history, acknowledged the existence of the secret military site in the Nevada desert long known to alien aficionados as "Area 51," but officially known either as "Groom Lake" or "Homey Airport." President Barack Obama also became the first president to officially mention the site that year, and in the years since, declassified documents have helped to present a better picture of the kind of research that went on in this facility from the 1950s to the present. The facility is still active, and some sources claim that secret experimental technologies are still developed there. While the base is now about as far from secret as it is possible to be, it is still illegal for civilians to fly over the base, and access to the facility is restricted with the use of electrified fences, automated security systems, and armed guards.

Area 51 is located in the midst of Groom Lake, a dry lake bed located around 130 kilometers north of Las Vegas, in an otherwise unused and inhospitable bit of desert. The site is part of a much larger group of military facilities covering about 2.9 million acres, which also includes the Nevada test site where nuclear weapons have been frequently tested and the Nevada Test and Training Range, a facility used to train soldiers and test equipment.

Declassified data indicates that Area 51 was officially built in 1955, but some claim that the facility was active in the late 1940s. The intense secrecy surrounding the site was due to Cold War paranoia about Soviet spies and weapons. Over the years, a bunch of governmental organizations used the Area 51 facilities for research, including the US Air Force, the CIA, and the Atomic Energy Commission (AEC). Until the twenty-first century, the CIA and the Pentagon continued to deny the existence of the base or to admit that any experiments were conducted there, and this stubborn adherence to absolute secrecy created the legend of Area 51.[2]

As details of what occurred at Area 51 have become available, thanks to the Freedom of Information Act and journalistic investigations, a different picture is emerging. From the early 1950s to the 1990s, Area 51 and the other facilities in the area were the site of a number of top-secret experiments involving nuclear and surveillance technology.

One of the programs now declassified was Operation Plumbbob, a series of atmospheric nuclear tests conducted just outside Area 51 in 1957. Among other things, the tests conducted during this operation involved simulating aircraft crashes. UFO sightings in the area around Nevada spiked during the time that this operation was ongoing, indicating that residents nearby may have been seeing the flashes of aerial explosions, or possibly even catching a glimpse of experimental vehicles being used in tests.

Beginning around 1955, the CIA used Area 51 and its runways to construct and test versions of the Lockheed U-2, also simply known as the "U-2 Spy Plane." A mishap with this vehicle created a major controversy that set back US and Soviet relations for decades, but before this happened, the CIA was testing this strange, alien-looking craft in the skies above Nevada, inspiring many "UFO" sightings and rumors of strange aerial activities surrounding the site. The subsequent Oxcart Program involved similar technology, specifically the Lockheed A-12 spy plane, which was also tested at Groom Lake in the early 1960s and inspired reports of possible alien vehicles around Nevada and in surrounding states. Many other surveillance and stealth aircraft were tested at the facility, and the vast deserts nearby used for nuclear testing were used in aircraft bomb and flare tests and many other types of experiments, many of which contributed to the perception of alien activity in the Nevada desert.[3]

The Roswell Connection?

The Roswell incident of 1947 involved an alleged UFO sighting followed by the discovery of debris by a rancher in Roswell, New Mexico. Witnesses claimed to have seen a saucer-shaped craft and the bodies of small individuals who looked like aliens. The government claimed that the wreckage found was the remains of a weather balloon and that there were no bodies found at Roswell, but the CIA and the Pentagon investigation helped to inspire rumors of a government cover-up. Over the years that followed, scattered reports and witnesses fueled these rumors with stories of seeing strange beings or technology in or around the base.

Then, in 1989, a man named Bob Lazar claimed that he had worked at Area 51 and had seen both alien technology and medical photographs of aliens. Lazar rapidly became one of the most famous figures in UFO legend as newspapers and radio stations covered his story. Later, Lazar added fuel to the fire when he contacted the media to claim that the government had raided his home and had engaged in other methods to intimidate and silence him. In an interview, Lazar even claimed that the US government had erased his educational records from CalTech and MIT. After a series of interviews and investigative pieces, Lazar claimed he had been asked to reverse-engineer an alien fuel, called "element 115."

Another major boom in Area 51 interest came after Journalist Annie Jacobsen published her 2011 book *Area 51: An Uncensored History of America's Top Secret Military Base.* Most of the book is a sober, journalistic account of data available through many declassified sources, but at the end of the book, Jacobsen included a series of claims that she obtained from a secret, anonymous source who was supposedly an engineer working in Area 51. According to Jacobsen's source, the CIA *did* actually uncover a "flying saucer" in New Mexico and brought the wreckage to Nevada in 1951, which is the reason that the facility got its name. According to Jacobsen's secret source, the machine contained two Soviet pilots who may or may not have been teenagers or young adults, but were "child sized." Jacobsen's source claimed that the Soviet aviators had been altered to look like aliens and the source believed that the Russians hoped to create an extraterrestrial panic that would distract the United States and give more time for the Soviet Union to develop nuclear technology.[4]

Jacobsen's book was not well received by journalists and specialists in military/intelligence agency history, but it became a massive bestseller, reinvigorating the discussion about Area 51. However, because Jacobsen's claims, which many experts in the field characterized as suspect and unrealistic, did not confirm the involvement of extraterrestrial technology, UFO enthusiasts did not embrace Jacobsen's work, preferring to believe that the site had been used to conceal alien bodies or technology rather than the bodies of Russian pilots involved in a 1940s military hoax.

Then, in 2017, in the midst of a documentary being filmed about Lazar's life, his home was raided by local police and the Federal Bureau of Investigation (FBI). Lazar claimed that the government was trying to recover samples of "element 115" that Lazar suggested he might have taken from Area 51. Investigative journalists later uncovered that Lazar's home had been raised because Lazar and his wife operated a business selling chemicals for scientific experimentation and study, which included several highly poisonous and toxic substances. One was called "United Nuclear Scientific," which was thallium sulfate, a tasteless, odorless substance that is frequently used in the manufacture of glass and electronics but is also highly toxic and difficult to detect, which has made it a popular poison. The FBI raid was intended to recover Lazar's sales records in connection to a case involving Janel Struzl, a 31-year-old who had been killed by thallium poisoning.[5]

Lazar and other UFO enthusiasts have continued to insist in the veracity of Lazar's claims, though there has never been any corroborating evidence. The educational institutions Lazar claims to have attended insist that he was never a student and never received a degree, and Lazar has not provided diplomas or any evidence of any college education. Places where he claimed to have worked have denied that they employed him, and he has never provided any information to prove previous employment. Several investigative books have been written about Lazar, and none of the authors have located individuals who can confirm his claims about his education or work history. To believe Lazar's story, one must believe that the government has the influence and ability to guarantee the silence of the many hundreds of individuals that should be able to confirm his claims and, for this reason, Lazar's particular chapter in UFO lore provides an example of where conspiratorial thinking intersects with the world created by UFO enthusiasts.

The Raid that Never Was

In 2019, college student Matty Roberts created a Facebook event called "Storm Area 51, They Can't Stop All of Us." The description of the event makes it clear that the intention was humorous. Roberts claimed that "Kyles," internet slang for white men with anger management problems, would attack the base en masse, forcefully uncovering the alien secrets contained there. Roberts even wrote, in the description, that the event was intended as a joke and that he personally had no intention to storm the base. By the time of the scheduled event, on September 10, 2020, more than 2 million people had signed up to attend. The military was forced to respond, with the Air Force releasing a statement to the effect that anyone who attempted to enter a US Air Force training facility would be prevented from doing so.[6]

Fearing that attendees would actually show up and try to storm the facility, leading to violence, Roberts and friends tried to organize an alternative alien-themed festival in the nearby town of Rachel, Nevada, which has fewer than 100 permanent residents and survives largely because the town is close to Area 51. Many of the town's businesses and facilities are alien-themed, and the initial event was planned to include the A'Le'Inn, a small hotel and inn located in the city. With interest growing and the small town lacking infrastructure, there was concern that the arrival of thousands might turn into a crisis, so the party was moved to Las Vegas, where Budweiser offered limited-edition alien-themed beer. An alternative group, not affiliated with Roberts and company, planned an alternative event for the tiny town of Hiko, which is also nearby Area 51 and features a bunch of alien-themed businesses as well, including a gift shop called the "Alien Research Center." This event featured speakers from UFO enthusiast circles and was aimed at attracting individuals who genuinely believe in UFO visitation, including a visit from Bob Lazar.[7]

The parties in Hiko, Rachel, and Las Vegas weren't the "raid" on the Area 51 facility that some hoped for, but they demonstrated the tremendous interest that belief in this top-secret government test site still generates. One of the most interesting revelations from research into the secretive experiments that occurred at the site is the understanding that the CIA and the Air Force most likely consciously encouraged belief that the facility had been used to study alien technology and even alien bodies. As the facility became public knowledge, and became associated with the sporadic UFO trends of the 1940s to the 1960s, government agents may have encouraged those theories as a way of distracting the public from speculating about the real activities going on at the facility, experiments with technology and tactics with more national security relevance than flying saucers.

Works Used

Aguilera, Jasmine. "Area 51 Is the Internet's Latest Fascination: Here's Everything to Know About the Mysterious Site." *Time*. July 17, 2019. Retrieved from https://time.com/5627694/area-51-history/.

"Area 51 'Uncensored': Was It UFOs or the USSR?" *NPR*. May 17, 2011. Retrieved from https://www.npr.org/2011/05/17/136356848/area-51-uncensored-was-it-ufos-or-the-ussr.

Chokshi, Niraj. "The Area 51 'Raid' Is Today: Here's How It Spun Out of Control." *New York Times*. Sept. 14, 2019. Retrieved from https://www.nytimes.com/2019/09/14/us/storm-area-51-raid.html.

Eco, Umberto. *Foucault's Pendulum*. New York: Harcourt, 1988.

McMillian, Tim. "Bob Lazar Says the FBI Raised Him to Seize Area 51's Alien Fuel: The Truth Is Weirder." *Vice*. Nov. 13, 2019. Retrieved from https://www.vice.com/en/article/evjwkw/bob-lazar-says-the-fbi-raided-him-to-seize-area-51s-alien-fuel-the-truth-is-weirder.

Nevett, Joshua. "Storm Area 51: The Joke That Became a 'Possible Humanitarian Disaster.'" *BBC News*. Sept. 13, 2019. Retrieved from https://www.bbc.com/news/world-us-canada-49667295.

"The Oxcart Story." *Air Force*. Nov. 1, 1994. Retrieved from https://www.airforcemag.com/article/1194oxcart/.

Notes

1. Eco, *Foucalt's Pendulum*.
2. Aguilera, "Area 51 Is the Internet's Latest Fascination: Here's Everything to Know About the Mysterious Site."
3. "The Oxcart Story," *Air Force*.
4. "Area 51 'Uncensored': Was It UFOs or the USSR?" *NPR*.
5. McMillan, "Bob Lazar Says the FBI Raised Him to Seize Area 51's Alien Fuel: The Truth Is Weirder."
6. Nevett, "Storm Area 51: The Joke That Became a 'Possible Humanitarian Disaster.'"
7. Chokshi, "The Area 51 'Raid' Is Today: Here's How It Spun Out of Control."

More Than 1 Million People Agree to "Storm Area 51," but the Air Force Says Stay Home

By Bobby Allyn
NPR, July 15, 2019

Imagine throngs of people who have never met each other assembling in mid-September before dawn in a Nevada desert town to rush the entrance of Area 51 in search of aliens.

It is a fantastical idea conceived of as a joke on social media, but its popularity has spread fast. On Monday, the number of people who signed up for the tongue-in-cheek Facebook call to "Storm Area 51" exceeded 1 million.

And now, U.S. military officials say they are monitoring the situation.

"The U.S. Air Force is aware of the Facebook event encouraging people to 'Storm Area 51,'" an Air Force spokesperson told *NPR*.

"The Nevada Test and Training Range provides flexible, realistic and multidimensional battlespace to test and develop tactics as well as conduct advanced training in support of U.S. national interests," said the official, using the full name of a site that includes Area 51. "Any attempt to illegally access the area is highly discouraged."

According to the event's page, the plan is to "naruto run" toward the facility so the group can "move faster than their bullets," the event says. "Lets see them aliens."

The sprinting style is a reference to Naruto Uzumaki, a Japanese anime character who runs with his chest pointing forward and his arms jutting straight back behind him.

The event has all the makings of a ludicrous Internet joke, right?

"Yes, it sounds like a joke, but there apparently are some people who want to check out the joke," Connie West, the co-owner of Little A'Le'Inn (pronounced "little alien"), told *NPR*.

West's inn in Alamo, Nev., is the closest lodging site to Area 51. "About 26 miles from the runway," she says.

Since the Facebook event launched, her phone has been ringing incessantly with people looking to book a room. Her 10 rooms are now full for the day of the event,

Sept. 20, and she said most of
the people who made the res-
ervations asked her about the
Area 51 gathering.

West also has about 30
acres of land that she allows

The top-secret base is not accessible to the public, though it has become a tourist destination.

campers to book for $15 a night. And so far, about 60 people have committed to
pitch a tent on the day of the event, something she has never experienced on a day
not associated with an organized event like a marathon or a bike race, competitions
that happen in the desert near her inn.

"Apparently, people are taking it seriously," West said. "I think they're stupid if
they think they're going to get to the test site, but I'm gonna capitalize on it."

To her, that means selling at the inn's gift shop T-shirts, bumper stickers, coffee
cups and keychains, which of course feature a nod to the obvious.

"All featuring aliens and/or Area 51," West said.

The top-secret base is not accessible to the public, though it has become a tourist destination, with alien-themed outfits like West's not uncommon. Nevada even
renamed a state road "Extraterrestrial Highway" because of reports of UFO activity
along the road.

Conspiracy theorists have obsessed over Area 51 for decades, claiming the U.S.
government is hiding aliens and crashed UFOs at the site. In 2013, the CIA released a classified 1992 report in which the federal government acknowledged that
spy planes were tested there. Officials also admitted that Area 51, the place where
many sci-fi stories have been based, is a real-life government facility.

In May, the *New York Times* reported that Navy officials, in classified guidance,
described "unexplained aerial phenomena, or unidentified flying objects," stoking
anew theories about extraterrestrial life hiding at Area 51.

It is difficult to say how many of the event's million backers know it is a joke and
how many are really considering making a trek to Nevada, but most of the thousands of posts on the page seem to indicate that it is not serious.

"We are forgetting something very crucial," wrote Nick Prafke. "We need vape
lords to create a smokescreen to block out satellite and camera images."

The person who created the event page is a 20-year-old man from California who
would be identified only as Val. He wouldn't share his last name for fear the publicity around the event would lead to his being harassed.

"I just thought it would be a funny idea for the meme page," Val said via Facebook Messenger. "And it just took off like wildfire. It's entirely satirical though, and
most people seem to understand that."

Val told *NPR* that he'll "more than likely be there, but not for the intended purpose."

He has been talking "with some pretty great people" about planning a different
kind of shindig, perhaps something educational, though it was unclear what exactly
the lesson would be.

Whatever it is, Val said it is unlikely to include "sprinting through the desert at 3am."

Print Citations

CMS: Allyn, Bobby. "More Than 1 Million People Agree to 'Storm Area 51,' but the Air Force Says Stay Home." In *The Reference Shelf: UFOs,* edited by Micah L. Issitt, 69-71. Amenia, NY: Grey House Publishing, 2022.

MLA: Allyn, Bobby. "More Than 1 Million People Agree to 'Storm Area 51,' but the Air Force Says Stay Home." *The Reference Shelf: UFOs,* edited by Micah L. Issitt, Grey House Publishing, 2022, pp. 69-71.

APA: Allyn, B. (2022). More than 1 million people agree to "storm Area 51," but the Air Force says stay home. In Micah L. Issitt (Ed.), *The reference shelf: UFOs* (pp. 69-71). Amenia, NY: Grey House Publishing.

I "Stormed" Area 51 and It Was Even Weirder Than I Imagined

By J. Oliver Conroy
The Guardian, September 24, 2019

In the middle of the Nevadan desert, outside a secretive US military airstrip, I found the world's strangest social media convention.

Dozens of young, good-looking, often costumed people were running around filming each other with semi-professional video rigs. They were YouTube and Instagram stars–or, more often, aspiring stars–here to "storm" Area 51 for the benefit of their followers and free the aliens held captive within. Or at least film themselves talking about it.

Joining them was a ragged army of hundreds of stoners, UFO buffs, punk bands, rubberneckers, European tourists, people with way too much time on their hands, and meme-lords in Pepe the Frog costumes–all here because of the Internet, the ironic and the earnest alike, for a party at the end of the earth.

Three months earlier, on 20 June 2019, the podcaster Joe Rogan released an interview with Bob Lazar. Lazar is a cult figure in UFO circles; he claims to have studied flying saucers at Area 51, the classified air force base in Nevada where the US government is rumored–by some–to make secret contact with extraterrestrial beings.

Rogan's millions of listeners heard the interview.

One of those listeners was Matty Roberts, a college student, anime enthusiast and video gamer in Bakersfield, California. Inspired by the Rogan podcast, Roberts created a joke Facebook event: "Storm Area 51, They Can't Stop All of Us." According to the plan, people would meet in Rachel, Nevada–the closest town to Area 51–in the early morning of 20 September, then swarm the defenses and see for themselves if the government was hiding aliens.

Things snowballed. Within hours, the page had thousands of RSVPs. Within days it had more than a million. The air force warned that things would end badly for anyone attempting a raid. The FBI paid the hapless Matty Roberts a house call.

So he came up with a brilliant pivot: why not channel this momentum into a Burning Man-style music festival in the desert? He joined forces with Connie West, the operator of Rachel's sole inn and restaurant, to plan what they called Alienstock.

Then came the first schism. Scornful of the internet interlopers, the Alien

Research Center in nearby Hiko, Nevada, decided to host its own Area 51 event the same weekend–for serious ufologists.

Roberts and West pressed on. But the town of Rachel (population: 54) lacked the infrastructure to handle thousands of conspiracy theorists and gawkers descending on rural Nevada. The local authorities feared potential calamity: people dying of dehydration in the desert, angry landowners, madmen with guns.

On 10 September, nine days before the event, Roberts backed out. He wanted no involvement in a "Fyre Fest 2.0", he told the media. He accused West of being insufficiently prepared for the coming flood. Budweiser offered to sponsor a free, alternative Alienstock event in a "safe, clean" venue in downtown Las Vegas. Roberts urged people to go there instead.

West refused to cancel the concert in the desert. She'd already sunk thousands of dollars of her own money into the event, she told reporters as she held back tears. Alienstock would happen, she said, whether anyone liked it or not.

Now there were three rival events all happening on the same weekend–one in Las Vegas, another in Rachel and a third in Hiko. No one had any idea how many people were coming.

I came equipped with a duffel bag of Hawaiian shirts and a case of vape cartridges, which I hoped to use as currency in the event of civilizational collapse in the desert.

But the desert would wait. The "Area 51 Celebration" in downtown Las Vegas did not get off to a promising start. When I arrived, shortly after 7pm, the outdoor venue–heavily bedecked with glowing neon alien signage–was mostly empty except for cops and local newscasters. A DJ blasted dubstep to a bare dancefloor. The venue even had a swimming pool, bathed in green light and watched by a bored-looking lifeguard.

I feared it might be a long night. I ordered a whiskey-and-water; the bartender filled a plastic stadium cup to the brim.

Then people started trickling in. Everyone was wearing their best alien-themed rave attire: one woman wore a shiny, and discomfitingly rubbery, head-to-toe alien costume. Another had a Rick-and-Morty-patterned dress. Three men tore up the dancefloor in matching alien-motif onesies. Someone carried a sign that said GREEN LIVES MATTER.

I talked to two people who'd driven six hours from Tucson, Arizona, on a whim to attend. One was wearing a Flat Earth Society T-shirt, though he said it was ironic.

I spied Matty Roberts in the center of a swirling mass of people, holding court. He was wearing a Slayer hat and black T-shirt; his long, dark hair flowed majestically down his back. He looked like a heavy metal-listening, Mountain Dew-drinking samurai lord, surrounded by courtiers and supplicants. I fought my way over.

He was in high spirits. "I'm absolutely amazed at how things turned out, and it's incredible," he told me as he signed autographs. I opened my mouth to ask a follow-up question but he was swallowed up again by the crowd.

By around 9pm, there were a couple hundred people jerking spasmodically to dubstep.

A woman who introduced herself as Shereel ("C-H-E-R-Y-L") said she was happy to be at the rave but disappointed she couldn't make the event in the desert.

Inspired by the Rogan podcast, Roberts created a joke Facebook event: "Storm Area 51, They Can't Stop All of Us."

"This is the first time since Roswell that people like us are all coming together," she said. "Even if nothing happens, we tried."

The DJ interrupted his set to thank Matty Roberts and give a "special shout-out" to Bob Lazar. The crowd cheered.

A warm wind was whipping through the arena. As the wind buffeted us and the rave lights flickered overhead, you could almost believe a UFO really was about to descend.

The next morning I got in my rental car and headed north.

The outskirts of Las Vegas–casinos, strip clubs, endless billboards for personal injury lawyers–dropped away rapidly. Now there was just desert in every direction, stunning in its vastness and austere beauty. Mountains towered over the highway, surrounded by hilly plains of cacti and scrub.

Soon most human settlement was gone. There was nothing alongside the highway–no strip malls, no fast food joints, and, I noticed, worryingly few gas stations. I had at least two hours of driving ahead, though I knew I was going in the right direction: every vehicle I saw was a police car, an RV or a news satellite van.

As I drove I listened to rightwing talk radio, then Top 40, then country, then a Bible discussion call-in show, then some Spanish-language stations, then static. A talk station interviewed the mother of a police officer killed by an undocumented immigrant. Sean Hannity made fun of the climate strike, and every talkshow discussed the *New York Times'* recent, partly retracted accusation against Brett Kavanaugh. It was, they pointed out, yet another sign of bias in the liberal media.

The first gas station was bustling with people buying water and jerry cans of gas. In the parking lot there was a camper van marked "AREA 51–HERE WE COME".

Finally, two hours north of Las Vegas, I saw the exit for State Route 375–also known, since its formal renaming in 1996, as Extraterrestrial Highway.

The US government owns thousands of square miles of land in northern Nevada. The area is big enough, and empty enough, to detonate a nuclear bomb–which the government has, on hundreds of occasions.

The "Groom Lake airfield"–Area 51–is part of a massive complex of military installations. Their activities are classified and the skies above are restricted air space. Little is known about what goes on there, though the air force tests experimental stealth aircraft, which may account for some UFO sightings.

Of course, military pilots are themselves known to report seeing what they refer to as "unexplained aerial phenomena". (Even the *New York Times* has reported on it.)

In the 2000s, Congress established an "advanced aviation threat identification program" to study the problem. The program wasn't classified, but it "operated with the knowledge of an extremely limited number of officials", according to *Politico*. The then Nevada senator Harry Reid helped secure the funding.

That's the end of the history lesson. The reader is free to investigate further and come to their own conclusions.

On the way to Rachel, I stopped at the rival festival at the Alien Research Center in Hiko. It was heavy on souvenir sellers, though there were some hardcore ufologists. A group called the Mutual UFO Network (Mufon) gave me a pamphlet offering certification to be a "field investigator".

If anything, the ufologists were more the exception than the rule. I had expected most Area 51 Stormers to be conspiracy theorists, 4chan types, or people on the fringe political spectrum, but a lot—probably most—were normies on a lark, or foreigners in search of peak Americana.

Two young men—one Swiss German, the other Japanese—told me they were friends who'd met at an English as a second language program in New York. A group of Britons told me they'd been taking a road trip up the west coast, heard about the Area 51 business, and decided to take a detour.

This was a common theme: "*Well, I'd been thinking about taking a road trip anyway, sooo...*"

When my car turned the last switchback into the valley toward Area 51, the car radio, theretofore static, suddenly started blasting Smetana's Má Vlast in eerie, crystal-perfect sound. The aliens, it seemed, were classical music buffs.

Rachel came into view—a tiny, one-horse town besieged by cars and tents and camper vans. Including the cops, EMTs, festival organizers, and so on, there looked to be a couple thousand people—not the two million who had RSVP'd to the Facebook event, nor the 30,000 the sheriff feared, but more than I thought would follow through.

Contrary to the wild warnings about a Fyre festival 2.0, things appeared mostly under control. Festival marshals waved me along to an assigned lot.

My neighbors at the parking lot-slash-campsite were a punk band called Foreign Life Form. They weren't part of the planned music lineup, one Life Form explained as he ate Chef Boyardee room-temperature from a can, but when they heard about Alienstock, it seemed like fate. They were trying to find the concert organizer to get added to the billing. To help seal the deal they'd painted their faces and arms green.

My other neighbor, an erudite, joint-smoking history podcaster from Oregon, wore a T-shirt that said "Take me to your dealer". He and his son had had the shirts custom-made; the Life Forms were disappointed they couldn't buy some.

Getting to the actual entrance to Area 51 took another 20 minutes of driving on an unmarked, unpaved road. Clouds of chalk billowed behind the cars coming and going.

At the end of the road was a drab military checkpoint flanked by concertina wire and threatening signs. The sign prohibiting photography was clearly a dead letter.

Rotating shifts of law enforcement officers of every variety–sheriff's deputies, state troopers, game wardens, park rangers–kept a watchful eye on everything. They seemed relaxed, though, and looked like they were having as good a time as the ostensible Stormers. After all, this was an excuse for them to hang out at Area 51, too.

(To my knowledge, no one actually raided Area 51, besides the two Dutch YouTubers who had tried to sneak through the perimeter two weeks earlier and ended up in jail instead.)

In addition to YouTube vloggers and Instagram influencers, there were more than a few actual journalists. Watching them scurry around diligently with tape recorders reminded me that I needed to find a Quirky Character who could give On-Scene Color. A talkative UFO buff would be ideal but the other journalists had already claimed most of the good ones.

I couldn't avoid noticing a pair of men in huge, papier-mache Pepe the Frog heads. The vloggers loved them, and the Pepes enjoyed mugging for the cameras. "My God," a girl said, "they're *adorable*."

Under their frog heads, the Pepes were two young Latino guys from California. When I asked them what they thought of the frog's association with the alt-right, one seemed confused. The other nodded in recognition but claimed he just thought the symbol was fun.

He said, "It's all about the–"

"Memes," finished the other. They both laughed.

I asked if it wasn't weird for them, as Latinos, to embrace a symbol affiliated with white nationalists.

"Yeah, I mean, they're a little, like, extreme for me sometimes," one said. "But sometimes you feel like they're right about some stuff."

I said, "Like what?"

"Like clown world."

"What?"

"Clown world."

"What?"

"Like the idea that we're all living in a world of clowns," he clarified.

Tendrils of fog hung over Alienstock. The temperature was dropping fast and the sun was low and pink in the sky. The sunset was sublime but I had a long drive to my motel ahead and a sick feeling that I should have left half an hour ago.

I bade farewell to the history podcaster. He reminded me that the area was open grazing land. "Watch out for the steer," he said. "They go right out into the road."

The next morning I debated whether to squeeze in another trip out to Alienstock and couldn't quite find the willpower. It was time to get back to civilization, I decided. Or at least Las Vegas.

I stopped at the gas station in Alamo, near Rachel. The town felt hungover, and it still had a day to go. Most of the locals seemed unsure quite how to feel about the whole thing. It was a boon to the local economy, yes, but also a financial disaster for the county government. There were rumors that the district attorney was planning to sue Connie West, or Matty Roberts, or even Facebook.

Most, though, just seemed excited at the idea that their corner of the world might become something bigger than a gas stop on the way elsewhere.

Everyone vowed that next year, they'd be ready.

Print Citations

CMS: Conroy, J. Oliver. "I 'stormed' Area 51 and It Was Even Weirder Than I Imagined." In *The Reference Shelf: UFOs,* edited by Micah L. Issitt, 72-77. Amenia, NY: Grey House Publishing, 2022.

MLA: Conroy, J. Oliver. "I 'stormed' Area 51 and It Was Even Weirder Than I Imagined." *The Reference Shelf: UFOs,* edited by Micah L. Issitt, Grey House Publishing, 2022, pp. 72-77.

APA: Conroy, J. O. (2022). I "stormed" Area 51 and it was even weirder than I imagined. In Micah L. Issitt (Ed.), *The reference shelf: UFOs* (pp. 72-77). Amenia, NY: Grey House Publishing.

The Secret History of Area 51, Explained by an Expert

By Alex Ward
Vox, September 18, 2019

You may have heard about the viral meme that could lead to people to storming Nevada's famed Area 51 later this week in order to uncover the secrets of the mysterious US Air Force base.

It's an absurd (and incredibly dangerous) idea—the Air Force has warned that it will defend the facility vigorously but the impulse behind it is perhaps understandable. For decades, the American imagination has run wild conjuring up all sorts of conspiracy theories about what is really going on at the site.

Is it a place where the US government is hiding UFOs and aliens? Or is it just a boring military base? And if it's just a boring military base, *why is the US government so obsessed with keeping everything about it a secret?*

To get some answers without risking getting shot at by the US military, I called up Annie Jacobsen, author of the book *Area 51: An Uncensored History of America's Top Secret Military Base.*

To write the book, Jacobsen interviewed over 70 people who had first-hand knowledge of the secret facility, including 32 who lived and worked at Area 51. The result is basically the most comprehensive account of the history of Area 51 you can get without a super-high-level security clearance.

If anyone had answers for me, it was her. And boy did she. But she also left me with new mysteries I hadn't even known to ask about.

Our conversation, lightly edited for length and clarity, follows.

Alex Ward

Okay, let's get right to it: What is Area 51, really?

Annie Jacobsen

Area 51 was the birthplace of overhead espionage for the CIA. It's where the U-2 spy plane was first built back in the 1950s, and it's where the intelligence community has worked with its military partners and others to work on espionage platforms.

It's also a place where all elements of the Defense Department work on some of their most classified programs along with members of the intelligence community, of which there are many.

There's also an element of Area 51 where the CIA trains its foreign paramilitary partners in counterterrorism tactics. They do this out on the wilds of Area 51 because they can bring some foreign fighters there who would otherwise not be welcomed into the country.

So the US can fly them in a plane with the windows drawn, drop them off, train them, and neither the fighters nor the American public have any idea where they were or what was going on.

Alex Ward

How important has Area 51 been to developing America's spying capabilities?

Annie Jacobsen

We would not have the kinds of incredible overhead espionage technology that we have today without the existence of Area 51. It allowed the different wings of the federal government to pursue technologies in a very large open area that they could otherwise not pursue.

The U-2 spy plane flew at 70,000 feet and 500 miles an hour. Think about how much work you would have to do to make something like that—it was this incredibly delicate plane. Pilots died out there testing it.

But it taught the powers that be that with this incredible effort of testing, you could achieve radical technologies.

Alex Ward

Why did this place become such a hotbed for spying technology and training? Is it just because it's so remote and so big?

Annie Jacobsen

When the base was founded back in the early 1950s, President Eisenhower tasked a guy named Richard Bissell from the CIA to find the most remote, most secretive place in the United States where they could work on the U-2 spy plane away from any prying eyes—Soviet or otherwise.

So Bissell smartly flew around with another CIA fellow and found the perfect fulfillment of that presidential request: a secret base centered around a dry lakebed in the middle of Nevada, located inside an already classified facility where the government was exploding nuclear weapons.

There was no way, Bissell realized, that anyone was going to try to get into this facility. Why would they want to? There were bombs going off!

Alex Ward

Everything about Area 51 screams secrecy—not just the location, but those who work there are brought into a very secretive culture in which it's extremely taboo to divulge anything. So how did the UFOs and aliens narrative come about?

Annie Jacobsen

Well, it remained obscured to the outside world until the late 1980s, when an engineer named Bob Lazar went on a local Nevada news program and stated that he had worked at Area 51 on a flying saucer that he believed had come from outer space. Bob Lazar also told the public he thought he saw an alien.

That was the moment Area 51 became a public fascination. It had been completely cloaked in secrecy before that.

And in all the decades since, interest in the site has gained momentum around two ideas: the theory that the US military has been reverse-engineering UFOs and alien technology at the site, and the truth about the base that some of the most remarkably advanced technology platforms have been created and tested out there.

Alex Ward

Why haven't any real secrets come out, though?

Annie Jacobsen

Bits and pieces of rumors would emerge over the decades, but the CIA had a very hefty disinformation and misinformation campaign going on out of Area 51.

The best example is in the 1950s when the U-2 spy plane was occasionally spotted. It basically looked like a flying cross way, way, way up high in the sky. And people would write to their Congressman and say, "I saw a UFO. Nothing flies this high." They were right in that regard. Nothing did fly that high, as far as anyone knew.

And so the CIA, as we know from declassified documents now, used that misidentification to their advantage. It let the UFO mythology evolve because it served as a useful cover for the secret base.

Alex Ward

Did the CIA propagate the aliens story, too?

Annie Jacobsen

I don't know of the CIA using the alien myth. I've never heard of it. But that's a great question; no one's actually ever asked me that.

Alex Ward

Okay, so we have this secretive testing site for overhead spy aircraft. What does this mysterious place actually look like?

Annie Jacobsen

Area 51 is part of the Nevada Test and Training Range, which is a large federal piece of property; it's roughly the size of Connecticut. Area 51 is a tiny parcel of land in that area that surrounds this dry lakebed. The exact dimensions obviously have never been reported, but you can hazard a guess based on looking at the map.

Area 51 was the birthplace of overhead espionage for the CIA. It's where the U-2 spy plane was first built back in the 1950s.

We know what happened from the 1950s through the 1970s, which was basically work on advanced aircraft for spying. But what gets very mysterious is what was going on in the 1990s and the 2000s, and certainly ever since the War on Terror.

I have absolutely no information about that. It's a jealously guarded secret, but you can be sure that whatever is being built and tested out there has evolved from the technology systems that were worked on before. We know the base is still flourishing despite people saying it's not.

The first president to state the word or phrase "Area 51" publicly was President Obama during an awards ceremony at the Kennedy Center. And when he did that, in essence, the words "Area 51" became declassified.

Alex Ward

The secrecy around Area 51 is surely what is making thousands say they want to storm that region. What will they see on the very off chance they try and succeed?

Annie Jacobsen

I couldn't even begin to speculate on whether or not anyone could get into Area 51 to see what's going on because it's fundamentally impossible. To think that the government isn't uniquely aware of everyone who goes anywhere near that facility is naive. A group of people massing anywhere near that facility is not going to happen. Local law enforcement would step in in a preemptive manner far before that happened.

Alex Ward

When people ask you to divulge some of the secrets you learned from Area 51, what do you tell them?

Annie Jacobsen

Well, first I send them to my book, of course.

Separate from that, I have interviewed scores of very smart, very highly placed government personnel who visited the base and believe the technology they saw is so advanced that they question whether or not it's manmade. That's intriguing to me. I don't report on that because there is no documentation to support that claim, but that is the opinion of many people that I know.

Alex Ward

To be clear, these are people who worked on these programs?

Annie Jacobsen

No, these are individuals who have visited the base and have been asked their expert opinion and analysis on classified programs.

Alex Ward

Just based on that, if someone were to ask you — and I guess that someone would be me — would you say with 100 percent confidence that there is no out-of-this-world technology being worked on at Area 51?

Annie Jacobsen

I report my books based on what qualified, competent, multi-sourced individuals tell me, and then I strive to back up information based on declassified documents that exist on the record. So I steer clear of reporting things that are observed but can't be verified.

Alex Ward

Fair enough, though that's fascinating to me.

What also intrigued me about what I learned from your book is that Area 51 seems like the quintessential Cold War location. Almost movie-like. It seems to have maintained that ethos, especially the drive to have the best technology and the guarded secrecy around such efforts.

Annie Jacobsen

That's a great observation on your part, and I believe speaks to the broader secrecy campaign at work in Area 51's favor. One could argue that all this business of captured UFOs from outer space and aliens is terrific chatter, right? "Look over here!" And people get to think, "Oh, Area 51 is just a Cold War relic."

My suspicion, though, is that some of the most cutting-edge science and technology programs are being tested at Area 51 today. We won't know about them for decades. But years from now the future technology that was being built there during the War on Terror will look quaint. Anachronistic. Outdated.

Alex Ward

That is my real fascination with Area 51. Yes, there's the UFOs and alien stuff, but it's possibly a very important epicenter for the future of American defense, of technological progress.

The life-or-death moments in America's future are, if not being seeded at Area 51, they're in a sense being decided there. To me, that's a great story in and of itself.

Annie Jacobsen

That was beautifully said. There's your closing paragraph. You don't need me. That was perfect.

Print Citations

CMS: Ward, Alex. "The Secret History of Area 51, Explained by an Expert." In *The Reference Shelf: UFOs,* edited by Micah L. Issitt, 78-83. Amenia, NY: Grey House Publishing, 2022.

MLA: Ward, Alex. "The Secret History of Area 51, Explained by an Expert." *The Reference Shelf: UFOs,* edited by Micah L. Issitt, Grey House Publishing, 2022, pp. 78-83.

APA: Ward, A. (2022). The secret history of Area 51, explained by an expert. In Micah L. Issitt (Ed.), *The reference shelf: UFOs* (pp. 78-83). Amenia, NY: Grey House Publishing.

Declassified: The CIA's Secret History of Area 51

By J. Dana Stuster

Foreign Policy, **August 15, 2013**

Area 51 is a touchstone of America's cultural mythology. It rose to notoriety in 1989, when a Las Vegas man claimed he had worked at the secret facility to discover the secrets of crashed alien hardware, spawning two decades of conspiracy theories and speculation about little green men. But the facility's history—and the history of the strange, secret aircraft that were developed there—extends back to 1955. Since its inception, the government has obliquely acknowledged its existence only a handful of times, and even the CIA's 1996 declassified history of the OXCART program— the development of the SR-71 Blackbird at the secret site—refers only to tests conducted in "the Nevada desert." The government has never publicly discussed the specific facility … until now.

On Thursday, the National Security Archive reported that it had gotten its hands on a newly declassified CIA history of the development of the U-2 spy plane. The report, obtained under the Freedom of Information Act, contains the CIA's secret record of how Area 51 came to be.

In 1955, CIA Special Assistant for Planning and Coordination Richard Bissell, Col. Osmund Ritland, an Air Force officer working on the U-2 project, and Lockheed aircraft designer Kelly Johnson began looking for a location in California or Nevada to test the U-2 prototype. The location had to be remote—far from the view of the public (or potential Soviet spies). On April 12, 1955, they were scouting locations from the air with the help of Lockheed test pilot Tony LeVier. While flying over the Groom Lake salt flat, they noticed an airstrip that had been abandoned after being used by the Army Air Corps during World War II. The CIA history describes their first encounter with the site:

> After debating about landing on the old airstrip, LeVier set the plan down on the lakebed, and all four walked over to examine the strip…. From the air the strip appeared to be paved, but on closer inspection it turned out to have originally been fashioned from compacted earth that had turned into ankle-deep dust after more than a decade of disuse. If LeVier had attempted to land on the airstrip, the plane would probably have nosed over when the wheels sank into the loose soil, killing or injuring all of the key figures in the U-2 project.

The salt flat and old airstrip were added to the Atomic Energy Commission's Nevada Test Site, which the land abutted. On the AEC maps, like the one above, the area was designated "Area 51." For the U-2 developers, it went by a different name.

> **The salt flat and old airstrip were added to the Atomic Energy Commission's Nevada Test Site, which the land abutted. On the AEC maps, the area was designated "Area 51."**

Johnson, the plane's lead designer, called the facility Paradise Ranch, and it came to be informally known as "the Ranch"—or "Watertown Strip," after bouts of flooding. The site became operational three months later, in July 1955, and testing of the spy plane was underway by the end of the month.

The UFO sightings began almost immediately. The U-2's operating altitude of 60,000 feet was higher than any other aircraft at the time—higher than some people even thought possible. "[I]f a U-2 was airborne in the vicinity of the airliner [during twilight hours] … its silver wings would catch and reflect the rays of the sun and appear to the airliner pilot, 40,000 feet below, to be fiery objects," the CIA history notes. These sightings were reported to air-traffic controllers and the Air Force, and were compiled in the Air Force's Operation BLUE BOOK, another subject of decades of alien conspiracy theories. "U-2 and later OXCART [the SR-71 development program] flights accounted for more than one-half of all UFO reports during the late 1950s and most of the 1960s," according to the CIA.

The Ranch was evacuated in June 1957 for a series of nuclear tests "whose fallout was expected to contaminate the Groom Lake facility," the report notes, but by September 1959 the CIA was back, using the site to develop the A-12, the forerunner to the SR-71. Over the next year, flights shuttled work crews to and from Area 51; the runway was lengthened, new hangars and 100 surplus Navy housing buildings were installed, and 18 miles of highway to the site were resurfaced. The facility seems to have remained in operation since.

The latest declassified documents aren't exactly new revelations for Area 51 scholars—much of this is known from interviews and inferences. In researching this article, I spoke to Bill Sweetman, an expert on secret U.S. military projects, who recounted the story of Bissell, Ritland, Johnson, and LeVier finding the site in the same detail as the declassified history. Sweetman directed me to the work of Chris Pocock, who has been reading between the lines of the CIA's redactions for decades. But the new report, all 355 pages of which you can read here, does tell a fascinating story about the origins of one of America's great mysteries.

Print Citations

Stutser, J. Dana. "Declassified: The CIA's Secret History of Area 51." In *The Reference Shelf: UFOs,* edited by Micah L. Issitt, 84-86. Amenia, NY: Grey House Publishing, 2022.

Stutser, J. Dana. "Declassified: The CIA's Secret History of Area 51." *The Reference Shelf: UFOs,* edited by Micah L. Issitt, Grey House Publishing, 2022, pp. 84-86.

Stutser, J. D. (2022). Declassified: The CIA's secret history of Area 51. In Micah L. Issitt (Ed.), *The reference shelf: UFOs* (pp. 84-86). Amenia, NY: Grey House Publishing.

This Man Saw Aliens in Area 51

By H. Dogar
Medium, May 16, 2021

Since its inception, Area 51 has been the subject of many controversies and conspiracies. In September 2019, a Facebook event called "Storm Area 51, They Can't Stop All of Us" went viral.

Allegedly, a hub for UFOs and aliens, it is a top-secret US military base in Nevada. What goes on in there is open to speculation and only known to a selected few.

Creation of Area 51

Area 51 was created on April 12, 1955, by CIA Director Allan Foster Dulles during the Cold War as a testing facility for reconnaissance aircrafts such as U-2 and SR-71 Blackbird.

The first president to publicly acknowledge its existence was Barack Obama (D-Illinois) in 2013. Before 2013 government officials did not acknowledge that any such facility existed.

There is little to no official information regarding the activities that take place there. However, it is assumed that the US is developing cutting-edge aircrafts and other technologically advanced war machines inside Area 51.

Conspiracy Theories

The clandestine nature of the project is the reason Area 51 has garnered the attention of the public. Among the most popular theories regarding Area 51 is the existence of extraterrestrial beings and UFOs there.

People claim that an alien spaceship crashed in 1947 at Roswell, New Mexico. Since then, that spacecraft and alien bodies are experimented on and kept hidden in the military base.

At first the US military thought that the supposed alien spaceship was actually an alien aircraft. However, later they declared it a weather balloon. To this day, people are not convinced by the weather balloon theory.

Bob Lazar—The Man Who Saw Aliens in Area 51

In 1989, a man named Bob Lazar came forward with his story and made the most audacious assertions.

According to Lazar, alien technology was being reverse-engineered in Area 51, and he used to be employed as a senior staff physicist in the US air force. He claimed to have

> **The most critical and relevant proof Lazar provided was the discovery and use of Element 115.**

worked with alien technology at a base called S4 near Area 51.

He observed many strange phenomena happening there. His job was to understand and analyze alien spaceships. He was given plans for a certain craft which was found in an archaeological dig.

At the base, no one was given the entire details of the craft they were working on. Information was given on specific parts they were working on. Bob's job was to study propulsion.

> *"Totally impossible. The propulsion system is a gravity propulsion system. The power source is an anti-matter reactor. This technology does not exist at all."*—Bob Lazar

He also claimed to have seen alien beings. He claimed that once when he was walking back to his workspace he saw an alien being in one of the rooms in Area 51. The figure was dark and had a large head.

He said that the ship they were working on would be tested at midnight by the air force. Once he found this out, he invited some of his friends to observe whatever was going on.

After his employer found this out, he was immediately fired. It was these outrageous statements of his that brought Alien theories to life.

Was Lazar Telling the Truth?

At first, Lazar refused to disclose his real name, but then, he decided to come out to the public for his own safety and became a part of the documentary *"Bob Lazar: Area 51 and Flying Saucers."* It was this documentary that led him to become a prime figure regarding Area 51 conspiracy theories.

What makes Lazar's claims sound legitimate is the fact that before his assertions, no one knew what happened in Area 51 at all. His claims made sense because it has been unveiled that aircraft such as the B-2 Stealth Bomber were created and developed there.

The B-2 Stealth bomber is a very unusual aircraft in design and shape. It looks like an alien war machine to some

Also, Lazar described the process, and scanning procedure one had to go through to enter the base, and the air force revealed that such techniques were indeed in use at the time Lazar was employed.

However, the most critical and relevant proof Lazar provided was the discovery and use of Element 115. At the time Lazar came forward with his story, this element did not exist.

It was only after 2003 that Russian scientists synthesized Element 115 artificially in their laboratory and named it Moscovium. Russia also has a highly developed space program of its own. This proves this theory that it is possible to obtain Element 115 from some extraterrestrial source.

Problems with Lazar's Story

Behavioral analysts and interviewers have observed that Lazar had a hard time keeping his story straight. He changed several details when he recounted the events in interviews, and this makes his credibility dubious.

Also, his educational and employment record, in his words, seems to be quite remarkable, but when a background check was run on him, it was found that the schools and employers he mentioned had no record of him.

Parting Thoughts

There is no conclusive evidence or report of what happens in Area 51. The US military and the CIA might be benefiting from the hype around Area 51 as an alien facility, because they can carry out their operations confidentially with this distraction.

Nonetheless, these paranormal stories and myths are both entertaining and mind-boggling.

Print Citations

CMS: Dogar, H. "This Man Saw Aliens in Area 51." In *The Reference Shelf: UFOs,* edited by Micah L. Issitt, 87-89. Amenia, NY: Grey House Publishing, 2022.

MLA: Dogar, H. "This Man Saw Aliens in Area 51." *The Reference Shelf: UFOs,* edited by Micah L. Issitt, Grey House Publishing, 2022, pp. 87-89.

APA: Dogar, H. (2022). This man saw aliens in Area 51. In Micah L. Issitt (Ed.), *The reference shelf: UFOs* (pp. 87-89). Amenia, NY: Grey House Publishing.

Out There

By George Knapp
Nevada Public Radio, **November 1, 2014**

A buzz was building inside the Kulturhuset, a community center built on Islands Brygge, the historic property on the waterfront of Copenhagen's harbor. Inside the hall, an audience of more than 120 Danes, Norwegians, Germans and Brits were waiting to hear about a mystery that first surfaced on Las Vegas television 25 years ago. What's the latest about Area 51, they wanted me to tell them—and whatever happened to that flying-saucer guy Bob Lazar?

Few people know better than I do how outlandish the Lazar story sounded when his tale of a secret Nevada base housing UFOs exploded onto the scene back in November 1989. To this day, it is still a bit befuddling to me that educated professionals, artists, musicians and retirees from all around Europe would gather to hear the latest scuttlebutt about the flying saucers supposedly housed in a secretive facility in the Nevada desert.

The Exopolitics Denmark conference, a two-day gathering in October, wasn't the first to focus on the subject, and it won't be the last. Area 51 is known around the world. Every day I receive letters, emails or phone calls from curious people in Ecuador, Iceland, Hong Kong, Russia or other far-flung places asking about Area 51 or the bookish whistleblower who put it on the map.

And that's exactly what Lazar did. Today, Area 51 is an oxymoron of the highest order—the world's best-known secret base. It has been mentioned in such blockbusters as *The Da Vinci Code*, *National Treasure*, an *Indiana Jones* sequel and *Independence Day*, in which Earthlings used the base to fight off an alien invasion. It's been featured in X-Files episodes, inspired dozens of books, hundreds of magazine articles, songs, cartoons, poems and business enterprises.

Earlier this year, former President Clinton talked about his interest in aliens and Area 51 on the *Jimmy Kimmel Show*. President Obama became the first sitting president to mention the name of the base during a ceremony honoring Shirley MacLaine.

Heck, even the Kardashians visited the outskirts of the base for their reality show.

There are several businesses named after Area 51—a rock 'n' roll band, a couple of bars, a video game, a fireworks company, jerky stores, inflatable love dolls, a dance troupe, art exhibits and the Las Vegas triple A-baseball team. After my first televised interview with Lazar, the most prominent business in Rachel, Nev., wisely changed its name from the Rachel Bar and Grill to the Little A'Le'Inn, selling T-shirts, posters, Groom Lake wine and Bob Lazar Christmas tree ornaments, along with "Beam Me Up, Scotty" drinks at the bar and Alien Burgers in the kitchen.

The story as told by Lazar has not only persisted but has blossomed, despite overtly hostile treatment by major media outlets and some of the best-known honchos of Ufology. Many of my journalism colleagues have worked their ink-stained panties into pretzel-thick bunches by fretting about the story. Nonetheless, since the saucer stuff burst into the public consciousness, every major media organization, program and paper in the world has, sometimes reluctantly, beaten a path to Area 51's once-obscure door. The attention has irritated some of my fellow reporters to the breaking point.

The Nonexistent Military Base

"Sometimes I really do regret it." On the media screen inside the Denmark hall, attendees are intently watching an edited clip of an interview with Lazar. "I almost feel like apologizing to them, saying, 'I'm sorry. Can I have my job back?'"

It's far too late for that—assuming he ever had a job out there in the first place. Whatever anonymity Area 51 enjoyed evaporated forever the moment Lazar spoke into a TV camera.

That first interview was broadcast in May 1989. Lazar's face was hidden and he used a pseudonym, Dennis. He claimed he worked intermittently at a location called S-4, south of Groom Lake, the main facility of Area 51. He said nine aircraft hangars had been built into the side of a mountain, adjacent to Papoose dry lake, disguised to look like the desert floor. Inside were nine flying saucers of alien origin. "Dennis" said the program was controlled by the U.S. Navy and that he and other scientists were taking the saucers apart to figure out how they worked—"reverse engineering," he called it.

Eight months later, on Nov. 10, KLAS-TV identified Lazar by name and showed his face as part of a series called *UFOs: The Best Evidence*. To this day, it ranks as the highest rated, most-watched local news program ever produced here. Within days, Lazar's claims had spread to Europe and Japan. TV crews and tabloid outfits flocked to Nevada. Tour buses filled with UFO enthusiasts staked out the deserts of the Tikaboo Valley. The guards, nicknamed "camo dudes," who patrol the perimeter of Area 51 were overwhelmed by all the attention, and ticked off, too.

Before that first broadcast, the only people familiar with the name of the base were folks who worked there or at the Nevada Test Site, or who lived in one of the remote communities of central Nevada. A few journalists had written bits and pieces about the base in the '60s and '70s. Aviation magazines speculated about spy planes that might be flying out of Groom Lake: the sleek SR-71 Blackbird, the gangly and magnificent U-2 and a strange craft rumored to be nearly invisible to radar. Among the handful of Nevada journalists with an interest in the base were two Las Vegas muckrakers, Bob Stoldal and Ned Day, who years later would become my bosses.

Acting on a tip from a former CIA pilot and Area 51 watcher named John Lear, Day and Stoldal broke a big story about the existence of the stealth fighter, which, they reported, had been developed and tested at Area 51. Federal lawmen hauled Day in for questioning about the source of his information. Stoldal was nabbed by military security on the outskirts of the base. In the early '80s, when they hired me to work at KLAS-TV, they told me intriguing stories about the ominous military base known by many names—The Ranch, The Box, The Watertown Strip and, best of all, Dreamland. By then the base had vanished from maps of the Test Site. The government began to pretend it didn't exist, even though it had been acknowledged by the military as early as 1955 and had been photographed by Russian satellites. It became readily apparent that intelligence agencies and the military were flat out lying to the public, and, as lies go, it wasn't very convincing.

"There Is No Delusion"

In Copenhagen, I told the audience that it no longer matters to me whether anyone believes Lazar's wild tale. (That's almost true.) For years after the story broke, it was a burning priority for me to try to convince the public—and my skeptical colleagues—that the story was legitimate and true. Not anymore.

These days, I focus on explaining why we took the story seriously in the first place, why we put our credibility on the line and how the tale subsequently took on a life that no one could have imagined. Like it or not, the Lazar meme is alive and well.

"Look, I'm not out there giving UFO lectures or producing tapes. I'm not in the UFO business," Lazar told me in an interview recorded this year at my home. "I'm trying to run a scientific business, and if I'm The UFO Guy it makes it really difficult for me. It is to my benefit that people don't believe the story. So when somebody says that they don't believe my story, I say, 'Great. Pass it around. I don't want you to believe it because it makes life difficult for me.'"

These days, he owns a scientific supply company in Michigan. He doesn't grant interviews and has done his best to put the whole episode behind him. He makes an occasional exception for me, mostly because of the strange road we have traveled together and the wars that have been fought in the odd little universe of Ufology.

"Look, I know what happened is true," Lazar says. "There is no doubt. Period. There is no delusion."

"Bob wouldn't go to the trouble to make up a story to lie to people and then perpetuate that lie," adds his close friend Gene Huff, a Las Vegas real-estate appraiser. "I mean, he lives in his own world and doesn't care what people think. Bob has no idea who won the Super Bowl last year, or the World Series. He's busy doing scientific stuff in Bob Lazar World and would not waste his time perpetuating a lie about UFOs."

When KLAS decided to pursue Lazar's claims, we spent eight months looking into his background and the larger story about UFOs at Area 51. On the surface, Lazar seemed an unlikely person to bring into such a sensitive program, assuming such a program exists. He likes machine guns and hookers, builds jet-powered cars, operated an outlaw-fireworks spectacular and flies a skull-and-crossbones flag over his house. Hardly the profile of a stuffy government scientist. What's more, the claims he made about places he worked and the school he attended could not be verified.

But instead of scaring us away from the story, the lack of records is what hooked us. Lazar said that prior to S-4, he had worked as a physicist on classified projects at Los Alamos National Lab in New Mexico. The lab told me it had no record whatsoever of Lazar. After I found a lab phone book listing his name, and a front-page Los Alamos newspaper article that named him as a lab physicist, Los Alamos still denied having any records. A headhunting company confirmed to me that it had hired Lazar to work at the lab and would send me copies of his records—but then clammed up, refusing to return phone calls or respond to letters, later denying it ever told me that it had the records.

I interviewed four people who had personal knowledge of Lazar working at Los Alamos on classified projects, and I even took a tour of the lab with Lazar as my guide. Something was clearly wrong with this picture. Later, after Lazar got into legal hot water, I asked Nevada Rep. Jim Bilbray for help tracking down Lazar's employment records. The congressman's office said it was stonewalled by several agencies and had never seen anything like it.

The second thing that hooked us was Lazar's knowledge of how things worked at Groom Lake. He says he spent very little time at Groom itself, but he knew, for instance, that a company called EG&G handled hiring. (Lazar claimed he had been sent to EG&G on a recommendation from physicist Edward Teller, whom he had met at Los Alamos.) Lazar knew that employees were flown to the base in unmarked planes or driven to Groom on buses with blacked-out windows — all true. He told us he had been interviewed by a guy who might have worked for the FBI as part of a background check for his security clearance. The agent's name was Mike Thigpen. As it turned out, Thigpen was a real person, but he worked for something called the Office of Federal Investigation, which conducts background checks on people hired to work at the former Test Site. That part of Lazar's story turned out to be true.

We also confirmed the existence of a location called S-4 on the Nellis range. There had been no references anywhere to such a place, but the public affairs office at Nellis confirmed to me that S-4 was a location at which the Air Force "tested certain equipment." (If you ask them today, they will tell you they are "unable to find any such designation on any maps" of the range.) How did Lazar know it existed?

The most important information Lazar had was the location and time of test flights of the saucerlike craft. Three weeks in a row, he escorted a group of people out to the desert east of the Papoose range, and they witnessed a glowing saucer-shaped object rise above the mountains and perform dramatic maneuvers. One of the sightings was captured on videotape. I interviewed each of the people who went along, and they told me the same story. Again, how did Lazar know? There had been no reports of aerial activity at Papoose. To this day, the official story is that the government has never had a facility at that location (even though satellite maps show a road leading from Groom Lake to the spot where Lazar says the hangars were located). As an aside, earlier this year, a UFO researcher found images on Google Earth that appear to show the outline of what could be nine hangar doors on the side of Papoose dry lake.

> **Area 51 is now permanently carved into the public consciousness.**

After an inconclusive result on one polygraph test—the examiner thought Lazar was too frightened—he easily passed a second test, administered an ex-cop named Terry Tavernetti, who quizzed him about his core claims. No attempt at deception was detected. Not long after we reported Tavernetti's findings, his office was burglarized and the charts from Lazar's test were stolen.

Yet another reason we gave Lazar the benefit of the doubt is that we found witnesses to back up at least parts of his story. I've interviewed more than two dozen people who worked at Groom Lake at various times from the 1950s through the '80s who have told me they saw saucerlike craft being tested or stored or taken apart in the vicinity of Area 51.

Most telling of all are those witnesses who were subsequently visited and threatened by various *Men in Black* types. Six people who offered to tell me their stories say they were visited immediately afterward and ordered to keep their mouths shut. If it had happened only once, I wouldn't think much about it. But these six people were solid citizens, not UFO nuts. One woman says she her life was threatened. Another man says he was warned about imprisonment if he talked. What this told me was that someone was listening to my phone calls. In the days before Edward Snowden's revelations, before we took for granted that the government is listening to every call and reading every email, this knowledge really pissed us off. Years after the story broke, I spoke to two former spooks who admitted that their job was to follow me, Lazar, Lear and Huff to see who we met or spoke to, at our workplaces, homes or bars. If Lazar's tale was baloney, why were we being followed?

Nonetheless, my approach to the Lazar material changed in the mid-'90s, for a couple of reasons. One is that I was concerned that I had crossed into advocacy instead of merely reporting on it. The fact is, it became personal. So many weird things happened during those first few years, things that are hard to explain if you weren't there.

Second, I reluctantly came to realize that I would never be able to prove Lazar's claims, no matter how many witnesses came forward to verify parts of his story. The folks who run Area 51 are simply better at this stuff than I am, and were always able to deflect stories about what goes on there. So I changed my focus to merely explaining how the story played out and why I remained interested over the years.

Amazing and Ridiculous

In the years since the stories broke, I've read the most amazing and ridiculous things about Area 51 and the saucer stories in local and national publications. Quite a few articles have poked fun at the story or at me. I've been the subject of at least three terrifically funny editorial cartoons in the *Review Journal*—all three now hang on my bathroom wall. The *RJ* media critic speculated that people were "rushing home at night to see my UFO reports" because they wanted to see the moment when I finally went "bull-goose loony on the air." One columnist bestowed on me the title of "grand mullah in the church of cosmic proctology."

Some of this stuff was pretty funny, but it bothered me that so many journalists had made up their minds about the Area 51 stories without ever doing a bit of work on it or without interviewing any witnesses. They seemed to know ahead of time, perhaps through psychic visions, that the story was bunk. To my mind, that isn't how journalism is supposed to work.

The most troubling failures by my colleagues has been their willingness to accept whatever stories are promulgated by the Air Force or CIA, as long as the end result is to poke fun at crazy UFO buffs.

In the years since the Lazar story broke, I've met scores of men who worked at Groom Lake on classified projects who have told me they never saw any saucers, and I believe them. But those same men have told me they would see co-workers in the chow line every day and never know what they were working on because they couldn't talk about it. They were reportedly ordered to lie about their work to their own spouses.

The other explanation that has been swallowed by those who don't want the story to be true is that maybe the tale told by Lazar is part of a disinformation plot, devised by the CIA or Air Force, as a way to distract attention away from something else flying around out there.

If that was the plan, it was a miserable failure.

As a result of the saucer tales, tens of thousands of people have made the trek out into the desert to watch the skies. Media crews are out there every week. Congressional investigators have asked tough questions. No one at Groom Lake ever wanted this much attention, regardless of what they are doing these days.

Critics of the story, or of Lazar, are welcome to laugh at it all they want. But the fact is, the debate is effectively over. Area 51 is now permanently carved into the public consciousness. Area 51 is now the yin to Roswell's yang, and the UFO stories are never going to be divorced from the base itself.

The UFO crazies won the battle. Long live Area 51.

Print Citations

CMS: Knapp, George. "Out There." In *The Reference Shelf: UFOs,* edited by Micah L. Issitt, 90-95. Amenia, NY: Grey House Publishing, 2022.

MLA: Knapp, George. "Out There." *The Reference Shelf: UFOs,* edited by Micah L. Issitt, Grey House Publishing, 2022, pp. 90-95.

APA: Knapp, G. (2022). Out there. In Micah L. Issitt (Ed.), *The reference shelf: UFOs* (pp. 90-95). Amenia, NY: Grey House Publishing.

UFOs, the Pentagon, and the Enigma of Bob Lazar

By Glen Meek
Nevada Current, June 1, 2021

This month, a highly anticipated report is slated to be delivered to the United States Senate on the subject of Unidentified Aerial Phenomena (UAP)—what we used to call Unidentified Flying Objects (UFOs). The report is to be made public (although it may have a classified annex) and was requested as part of the Intelligence Authorization Act attached to a COVID-19 relief bill. Its purpose is to provide lawmakers with the best information available from the Pentagon and the intelligence community about incidents that appear to involve vehicles with amazing flight characteristics far beyond those of our most advanced aircraft.

But, this report should also shed light on—and, in theory, resolve—a thirty-year old, major UFO puzzle with Nevada origins: did a young physicist named Bob Lazar actually work on captured extraterrestrial spacecraft at a secret government facility called S-4, in Lincoln County near Area 51?

Lazar surfaced publicly in 1989, when he was interviewed by my former colleague George Knapp of KLAS-TV, Las Vegas. At first, Lazar spoke only in silhouette, and used the pseudonym "Dennis". Later, he came forward under his own name and with no disguise. Lazar's claims were fantastic: that the U.S government had, in its possession, nine crashed or captive spacecraft from another world—at least one of them shaped like an actual saucer. Lazar claimed he'd been part of a team hired by the government to "reverse-engineer" the craft, which would unlock for American scientists the propulsion secrets they needed to pave a path to the stars.

Lazar said he was fired from his job at the clandestine military base because he brought some friends into the desert near Area 51 one evening to surreptitiously watch a saucer being test flown. A Lincoln County deputy caught the group leaving the area and the deputy ratted Lazar out to the government.

Lazar's story combined the most compelling elements of alien abduction stories and shadow-government conspiracy theories. The tale had a profound influence on popular culture from cartoons like *American Dad* to movies like *Paul & Independence Day.*

While publicity surrounding Lazar's amazing claims literally put Area 51 on the map, it also shined a spotlight on himself, and it wasn't long before people started picking apart his story. Places where Lazar claimed to have gone to college—like CalTech and MIT—said they'd never heard of him. About a year after his initial TV interview, Lazar found himself criminally charged for helping operate what prosecutors described as an illegal "high-tech whore house." That didn't help his credibility much.

As his case worked through the legal system, Lazar produced one of the few bits of physical evidence that he'd worked at a secret base in Nevada. It was a W-2 form, reflecting income of less than one thousand dollars, purportedly paid to him by the Department of Naval Intelligence.

Even that form was questioned over its authenticity. Skeptics pointed out that there's an Office of Naval Intelligence within the Department of the Navy—but not a Department of Naval Intelligence.

I covered Lazar's criminal case as a reporter for KTNV-TV in 1990. I remember him pleading guilty to pandering and I recall thinking: if his saucer stories were true, and he's typical of the scientists we have working on the most significant scientific project in history—then our planet might be in deep doo-do.

Yet, credibility issues aside, and despite a dearth of physical evidence and lack of corroboration from other scientists, Lazar's astounding tale has not only survived over three decades—but thrived.

His claims received renewed attention in 2018 thanks to a documentary produced by movie maker Jeremy Corbell. The documentary—widely viewed on Netflix—led to Lazar appearing on the Joe Rogan podcast, possibly the most popular podcast on the planet (this planet, anyway). Corbell, meanwhile, has been interviewed multiple times recently on network news talk shows. He is the source of at least one, recently leaked UAP video that depicts what appear to be triangular shapes moving through the sky.

Corbell—in the interviews I've seen—has not claimed the UAP videos show alien intelligence at work. But he did say in his documentary that he believed there was more evidence Bob Lazar was telling the truth than there was that he was lying.

Far be it from me to suggest these aerial objects could *not* be of extraterrestrial origin. They may very well be. But, I would caution people inclined to rule out earthly explanations not to jump to conclusions. Just because you don't know what something is doesn't mean it is what you wish it was. UK science writer Mick West has provided very plausible terrestrial interpretations of the most recent UAP videos making rounds on TV, including the video of flying triangles.

The request for the Senate UAP study makes no mention of alien intelligence or extraterrestrial space vehicles. But the language of the request calls for such a comprehensive study that the results should either confirm or debunk Lazar's claims.

The Director of National Intelligence, working with the Secretary of Defense and other agencies, is directed to provide a report that includes (in part):

> A detailed analysis of unidentified aerial phenomena data and intelligence reporting collected or held by the Office of Naval Intelligence, including data and intelligence reporting held by the Unidentified Aerial Phenomena Task Force.

A detailed analysis of unidentified phenomena data collected by:

1. geospatial intelligence;

2. signals intelligence;

3. human intelligence; and

4. measurement and signals intelligence;

A detailed analysis of data by the FBI, which was derived from intrusions of unidentified aerial phenomena data over restricted United States airspace.

Also to be included in the report:

Identification of potential aerospace or other threats posed by the unidentified aerial phenomena to national security, and an assessment of whether this unidentified aerial phenomena activity may be attributed to one or more foreign adversaries;

Identification of any incidents or patterns that indicate a potential adversary may have achieved breakthrough aerospace capabilities that could put United States strategic or conventional forces at risk.

Thus, the upcoming Senate report has the potential to paint Lazar as an unfairly maligned interstellar whistleblower with more impact than Edward Snowden, Karen Silkwood and Daniel Ellsberg combined—or suggest he's either a liar or a loon.

Assuming Lazar has been telling the truth—can the report avoid conceding that? Wouldn't the Pentagon have to say, at the very least, "Well, Senators, we're not sure what's causing all these recent UAP sightings, but we can tell you that we have an alien technology in our possession capable of performing the same kind of high-speed, gravity-defying maneuvers we're seeing in these videos."

Of course, such news would be the biggest story since Genesis.

I'm not getting vibes that a world-shattering revelation of that scale is about to be made. For example, former President Barack Obama, who was this nation's commander-in-chief and presumably should know what's going on, was asked point-blank about UFOs in a recent interview with CBS-TV's James Corden.

While Obama said he was aware of real incidents involving unknown objects in the sky making incredible, unexplained maneuvers—he also addressed the issue of aliens and captive alien spacecraft, saying:

"When I came into office, I asked (about aliens), right? I was like, alright, is there the lab somewhere where we're keeping the alien specimens and spaceship? They did a little bit of research and the answer was no."

So, if the upcoming Senate report does *not* vindicate Lazar, what *will* it say about him? Will he even be mentioned? Or mentioned as a mere minor player who made extraordinary claims but was an ordinary employee at Area 51 who never got near a saucer because there weren't any?

My suspicion is the report will contain new details about many incidents already reported, and new reports of other sightings that have been previously

> **At the very least, the government and military are finally taking a serious and urgent look at what's causing these phenomena and whether they pose a threat to our security.**

secret. There will likely be some events that seem to defy conventional explanation.

But, I think people who are expecting the military to finally provide evidence validating Lazar's resume as a saucer mechanic will be disappointed.

One thing you can say about Lazar after all these years: he was unequivocal. Lazar did not drop vague, tantalizing hints (as some have recently done in the media) that American scientists have possible "exotic materials" that need further testing to determine whether they're of alien origin. Lazar flat out said our scientists have nine captive alien craft (nine!), that they've been studying these craft for more than thirty years, and that he personally wrenched on the machines.

Based on Obama's comments, though, I don't think we'll see evidence of that in the upcoming report. And if Lazar's case remains unconfirmed, I fear true believers may decry the Senate report as just another whitewash, a 21st century redux of "Project Bluebook"—which looked at more than 12,000 UFO sightings between 1952 and 1969 and concluded there was no evidence any of them involved extraterrestrial vehicles.

At the very least, the request for the report indicates the government and military are finally taking a serious and urgent look at what's causing these phenomena and whether they pose a threat to our security. That's progress, and that's good.

But, if the report comes up short for those expecting proof-positive of alien contact, all I can say is this: the truth *is* out there. And watch the skies. Keep watching the skies.

Print Citations

CMS: Meek, Glen. "UFOs, the Pentagon, and the Enigma of Bob Lazar." In *The Reference Shelf: UFOs,* edited by Micah L. Issitt, 96-99. Amenia, NY: Grey House Publishing, 2022.

MLA: Meek, Glen. "UFOs, the Pentagon, and the Enigma of Bob Lazar." *The Reference Shelf: UFOs,* edited by Micah L. Issitt, Grey House Publishing, 2022, pp. 96-99.

APA: Meek, G. (2022). UFOs, the Pentagon, and the enigma of Bob Lazar. In Micah L. Issitt (Ed.), *The reference shelf: UFOs* (pp. 96-99). Amenia, NY: Grey House Publishing.

4
Alien Science

The scientific study of space and extraterrestrial life bears little resemblance to pop-culture images of aliens and flying saucers. Above, the Milky Way as viewed from La Silla Observatory in Chile.

The Scientific Study of Aliens and UFOs

If there is no evidence that aliens or UFOs exist, then are UFOs an appropriate subject for scientific study? There are several fields of human inquiry that are relevant to the study of UFOs and alien visitation. The study of extraterrestrial life in all forms is called "astrobiology," and it is a field with many subdisciplines and specialties. Astrobiologists create tools and studies to search for signs of life on other planets, consider evolutionary concepts and how they apply to extraterrestrial environments, and contribute to many other fields of space science. While astrobiology is the primary scientific discipline dealing with the possibility of alien life, there are other fields of academic inquiry that are also relevant, including engineering, computer science, psychology, and sociology.

Is There Life on Mars?

University of Chicago researchers Stanley Miller and Harold Urey conducted a series of now famous experiments in the early 1950s in which they showed how it was possible to recreate a synthetic environment similar to what might have existed in the early Earth and then to use that environment to create the building blocks of life. These experiments led to the development of a new field of inquiry, initially called "exobiology," but later named "astrobiology," in which scientists sought to understand the fundamental conditions needed to support the most basic manifestations of life. During the "Space Race," National Aeronautics and Space Administration (NASA), the foremost US civilian space agency, and the US Air Force conducted separate but similar experiments toward the goal of using various kinds of technology to explore space. NASA funded the organization's first astrobiology program in 1959, a probe designed to detect the fundamental building blocks of life that was intended to allow astronauts to search for signs of life outside the Earth's atmosphere.[1]

Perhaps the person most responsible for developing astrobiology into a serious scientific discipline was Harold "Chuck" Klein, a microbiologist who studied carbohydrate metabolism and headed the biology department at Brandeis University in Massachusetts. From 1960 to 1961, while Klein was spending a year as a visiting professor at the University of California, Berkeley, one of his students introduced him to the theories of Carl Sagan, who went on to become one of the most influential space scientists in American history and was an early proponent of the search for life outside of Earth. Klein learned that NASA was attempting to start an in-house life sciences program that would guide efforts to research and study life outside Earth, and Klein decided to apply. In 1963, Klein was chosen to oversee NASA's first Life Sciences Program at the organization's famed Ames Research Center (ARC).[2]

NASA's first major astrobiology study came in the 1976s, with the Viking lander's visit to Mars. Specialized equipment allowed scientists to sample the first couple of centimeters of Martian soil, which were used to try and grow microbes. The experiments failed to produce signs of life and NASA dramatically reduced funding for future astrobiology experiments as a result, but interest in space biology was revived in NASA in the early 1990s thanks to France Córdova, who was a chief scientist at Ames, Charles Kennel of the University of California, and Wesley Huntress, an administrator in space science for NASA. Huntress suggested changing the name of the field from exobiology to astrobiology, as the field was evolving to cover many subjects outside the initial life sciences focus represented by Ames. Space biology was thrust into the mainstream again in 1996, when NASA scientist David McKay and colleagues published a controversial article suggesting that signs of microbial life had been found in the remains of a Martian meteorite. Though the findings in the paper were later called into question by many other scientist and have since been considered likely an artifact of poor investigation rather than actual signs of Martian life, the 1996 paper generated tremendous national interest in astrobiology and NASA greatly increased investment in the field.

Interest in extraterrestrial life on Mars continued to play a role in the Mars rover programs, in which a series of semiautonomous vehicles were sent to Mars to conduct research. The 1997 Sojourner rover was followed by the Spirit rover, the Opportunity, the Curiosity, and the Perseverance rovers, each of which were outfitted with tools designed by researchers under the NASA Astrobiology Institute (NAI) program to search for signs of life on Mars. In one of NASA's most recent efforts, the curiosity rover used an innovative tool called the Sample Analysis at Mars (SAM) to dissolve samples of Martian soil, a technique known as "wet chemistry derivatization." The study allowed scientists to locate organic molecules, but it did not result in any concrete evidence of life on Mars.[3]

Life Beyond Mars

The search for life on Mars was one of the primary inspirations for NASA's first exobiology experiments and continues to play a major role in the science of astrobiology, but it represents only one arena of astrobiological research. One of the areas of inquiry in which research is needed is in the field of unidentified aerial phenomena (UAPs), better known in the United States as "UFOs."

From their inception, NASA scientists and administrators have been careful to distinguish between the scientific research conducted by NASA scientists and the public hunger for information on UFOs. Because there is no physical data to evaluate, nor substantive evidence to suggest alien visitation, NASA scientists have traditionally dismissed the search for UFOs as non-scientific, and scientists studying the possibility of extraterrestrial life have often endeavored to distance themselves from UFO and alien enthusiasts. However, attitudes about the relationship between science and UFOs are beginning to change. In 1968, Dr. Edward U. Condon of the Colorado Project reviewed cases of UFO sightings and argued that no serious scientific research into the subject could be justified by the limited evidence available to suggest that there was anything substantive to find. Thirty years later, a panel of scientists took another look at UFO data and claims and reached a very different set of conclusions. In a 1998 press release members of the scientific panel noted that some UFO sightings might indicate rare natural phenomenon of interest to climatologists and earth scientists and also argued that UFO sightings might be of interest to the fields of sociology and psychology, even if there was no evidence to suggest extraterrestrial involvement.[4]

In the 2010s, Americans learned that US Navy and US Air Force service members had seen more UAPs than had been previously revealed and that, in a number of cases, the sightings made by service members, utilizing technology that allowed for the evaluation of speed and trajectory, revealed seemingly impossible physical phenomena operating within Earth's environment. Some believe that these sightings show the operation of as-yet-unknown vehicles being operated by earthlings, but utilizing poorly understood technology, while others believe these sightings represent actual cases of alien visitation. In any case, the release of new declassified data on military UAP sightings, along with the 2021 Pentagon study on UAPs, indicates that scientific research into this field may be necessary to better evaluate and understand the phenomena in question.

Harvard University physicist Avi Loeb became one of the most high-profile scientists to suggest it might be worthwhile to invest in technology to search for extraterrestrial life within the solar system, even on Earth's surface. Leob's proposed "Galileo Project" would bring a number of rigorous scientific tools into the realm of UFO studies, including, for the first time, using NASA telescopes to study UFO claims as well as a network of telescopes that could be organized to better detect and evaluate any UAP located within the Earth's atmosphere. While considered something of a radical in scientific circles, a number of other members of the space science elite have come to the defense of Loeb's claims and have made similar arguments.[5]

Writing in *Scientific American*, Loeb said of his Galileo Project that

> a fresh scientific study that offers reproducible evidence for UFO sightings and resolves their nature would demonstrate the power of science in answering a question that is clearly of great interest to the public.

This quote reflects the idea that science should endeavor to answer not only questions that are productive in terms of resulting in discoveries with immediate human applications, but should also endeavor to answer questions that arouse popular interest. But Loeb also argues:

> Finding a conclusive answer on the basis of open data will enhance the public's confidence in evidence-based knowledge. Currently, the UFO mystery surrounding the expected inconclusive interpretation of the Pentagon report will fuel unsubstantiated speculations. A decisive scientific experiment holds the promise of clearing up the fog.[6]

Loeb's arguments here reflect the difficulty that scientists and educators have encountered with helping to influence public opinions on key policy issues involving scientific data. In the UFO debate, believers have frequently expressed the belief that the scientific and governmental establishment have hidden truths about aliens and UFOs from the public. The scientific community's effort to distance themselves from the cultural interest in UFOs may have encouraged the perception of a conspiracy between science and government and Loeb and allies therefore argue that openly investigating UAP sightings with scientific technology could help to dispel this myth while also answering interesting questions about the origin and nature of unexplained phenomena.

Whether Loeb's Galileo Project or similar efforts to utilize scientific tools to answer questions about UAPs might provide clarity, it will not dispel interest and belief in UFOs among some circles. However, the transformation of scientific thinking on this issue could provide useful information on a variety of topics, not least of which are the various sociological and psychological issues at play in developing belief and incorporating data into the public discourse on key issues. Even if the scientific study of UFOs only serves to better illustrate the factors that motivate interest in the topic, such research might be illustrative in other issues involving the intersection of information and belief.[7]

Works Used

Eghigian, Greg. "UFOs and the Boundaries of Science." *Boston Review*. Aug. 4, 2021. Retrieved from https://bostonreview.net/science-nature/greg-eghigian-ufos-and-boundaries-science.

"Harold P. Klein." *NASA*. NASA Ames Hall of Fame. 2021. Retrieved from https://history.arc.nasa.gov/hist_pdfs/bio_klein.pdf.

Hubbard, G. Scott. "Astrobiology: Its Origins and Development." *NASA*. Aug. 6, 2008. Retrieved from https://www.nasa.gov/50th/50th_magazine/astrobiology.html.

Loeb, Avi. "What We Can Learn from Studying UFOs." *Scientific American*. June 24, 2021. Retrieved from https://www.scientificamerican.com/article/what-we-can-learn-from-studying-ufos/.

O'Callaghan, Jonathan. "NASA's Curiosity Mars Rover Tests New Way to Search for Alien Life." *New Scientist*. Nov. 1, 2021. Retrieved from https://www.newscientist.com/article/2295603-nasas-curiosity-mars-rover-tests-new-way-to-search-for-alien-life/.

Salisbury, David F. "Scientific Panel Concludes Some UFO Evidence Worthy of Study." *Stanford*. June 22, 1998. Retrieved from https://news.stanford.edu/pr/98/980629ufostudy.html.

Shostak, Seth. "Harvard's Avi Loeb Thinks We Should Study UFOs—and He's Not Wrong." *Scientific American*. July 29, 2021. Retrieved from https://www.scientificamerican.com/article/harvard-rsquo-s-avi-loeb-thinks-we-should-study-ufos-mdash-and-he-rsquo-s-not-wrong/.

Notes

1. Hubbard, "Astrobiology: It's Origins and Development."
2. "Harold P. Klein," *NASA*.
3. O'Callaghan, "NASA's Curiosity Mars Rover Tests New Way to Search for Alien Life."
4. Salisbury, "Scientific Panel Concludes Some UFO Evidence Worthy of Study."
5. Shostak, "Harvard's Avi Loeb Things We Should Study UFOs—and He's Not Wrong."
6. Loeb, "What We Can Learn from Studying UFOs."
7. Eghigian, "UFOs and the Boundaries of Science."

Ufos Are an Intriguing Science Problem; Congress Must Act Accordingly

By Marik von Rennenkampff
The Hill, July 8, 2021

This description—which outlines an intriguing science problem—could easily apply to mysterious flying objects encountered by military aviators in recent years. In 2014 and 2015, for example, Navy pilots tracked unidentified craft seemingly able to turn, stop in midair and rapidly accelerate "with no jet engine, no exhaust plume" and no wings.

A few years earlier, at least five naval aviators witnessed an object that, as a squadron commander later recounted, had no "wings or rotors and outran our F-18s," accelerating to extreme speeds in the blink of an eye.

According to former director of national intelligence John Ratcliffe, unidentified objects are engaging "in actions that are difficult to explain. Movements that are hard to replicate, that we don't have the technology for, or are traveling at speeds that exceed the sound barrier without a sonic boom." Asked about these encounters, Sen. Mitt Romney (R-Utah) referred to "technology which is in a whole different sphere than anything we understand."

Similarly, former President Obama stated that "there's footage and records of objects in the skies, that we don't know exactly what they are. We can't explain how they moved." Obama's CIA director, John Brennan, went a step further, speculating that these mysterious craft might constitute "a different form of life."

But the description at the top of this column is not from a high-level government official or a pilot. Nor, despite similarities, does it describe any recent UFO encounters.

Instead, it is an excerpt from 1968 congressional testimony by the late James McDonald, a leading atmospheric physicist and professor of meteorology at the University of Arizona.

Initially a skeptic with only a tangential interest in UFOs, McDonald found his scientific curiosity aroused after discovering that official explanations for several noteworthy UFO sightings were absurdly unscientific.

After spending years combing through declassified documents and scrupulously tracking down more than 500 witnesses, McDonald became the world's premier scientific authority on UFOs. Perhaps most intriguingly, his archive of extraordinary, physics-defying UFO reports spanning the mid-1940s to the late 1960s has remarkable parallels to more recent incidents.

Unsurprisingly, McDonald's painstaking research turned him from skeptic to outspoken advocate of serious academic study of UFOs. But as an exasperated McDonald told Congress, the scientific community "has been casually ignoring as nonsense a matter of extraordinary scientific importance."

Testifying alongside McDonald at that 1968 hearing on UFOs was J. Allen Hynek, chair of the astronomy department at Northwestern University. Hynek, like McDonald, began his academic career a fierce UFO skeptic. But after two decades as a consultant to a U.S. Air Force project cataloguing UFO sightings, Hynek had seen enough compelling data to implore Congress and the scientific community to initiate a robust, fiercely independent academic inquiry into such encounters.

Today, scientists are generally dismissive of UFO reports. While most contemporary academics are unfamiliar with Hynek and McDonald's meticulous research, any scientist or skeptic would do themselves a service by reading Hynek's concise reflections on a 20-year career investigating the UFO phenomenon.

Hynek and McDonald were particularly struck by the sincerity, good judgment and professional caliber of hundreds of often-reluctant witnesses who had nothing to gain–and much to lose–by reporting UFO sightings. Moreover, McDonald and Hynek found that radar and other technical data corroborated credible eyewitness accounts in many of the most remarkable incidents. As Hynek observed, skepticism of the UFO topic is largely due to scientists' lack of exposure to such "really challenging UFO data."

> **Much of the aversion to serious investigations of these phenomena is rooted in the conclusions of a massive 1969 report funded by the U.S. Air Force.**

Moreover, much of the aversion to serious investigation of these phenomena is rooted in the conclusions of a massive 1969 report funded by the U.S. Air Force. Billed as the final say on UFOs, the 1,000-page report's summary claimed that "extensive study of UFOs probably cannot be justified in the expectation that science will be advanced thereby."

But this conclusion, written by physicist Edward Condon and reported by major media outlets at the time, did not reflect important scientific analysis in the report. In stark contrast to Condon's recommendation against academic study of UFOs, the American Institute of Aeronautics and Astronautics' scientific consensus held that "a phenomenon with such a high ratio of unexplained cases (about 30% in the Report itself) should arouse sufficient curiosity to continue its study."

McDonald, Hynek and several other experts also made abundantly clear that much of the so-called Condon Report was unforgivably flawed. It was biased from the outset, omitted important cases and critical context, relied on shoddy or nonexistent witness interviews and frequently ascribed absurd, unscientific explanations to extraordinary events.

As Stanford physicist Peter Sturrock noted, "critical reviews [of the report] came from those scientists who had actually carried out research in the UFO area, whereas the laudatory reviews came from scientists who had not carried out such research."

But for an academic community already wary of involvement in a topic associated with kooky UFO fanatics and bizarre works of science fiction, the report's overarching recommendation against rigorous academic study of UFOs was–as Hynek accurately noted–"the kiss of death to any further investigation." A half century later, little has changed. With few exceptions, the stigma largely remains.

Following the report's release, an exasperated McDonald spoke at a symposium organized by the American Association for the Advancement of Science, telling his colleagues that "science is in default for having failed to mount any truly adequate studies of [the UFO] problem." The audio recording of McDonald's AAAS presentation is a must-listen for any skeptical scientist.

A few years before writing the book that inspired the film *Close Encounters of the Third Kind*, Hynek drilled down to the root of the problem: "So powerful and all-encompassing have the misconceptions among scientists been about the nature of UFO information that an amazing lethargy and apathy to investigation has prevailed. This apathy is unbecoming to the ideals of science and undermines public confidence."

Make no mistake: These are remarkable statements from two academics who began their careers deeply skeptical of the UFO phenomenon.

With recent UFO encounters mirroring the incidents that stirred Hynek and McDonald's academic curiosity, Congress must continue to assert itself on an issue that begs for scientific investigation.

It can begin by following Hynek's recommendation to establish an independent "UFO Scientific Board of Inquiry, properly funded" and staffed by academic experts with access to relevant data. To alleviate national security concerns, sensitive information can be analyzed by Department of Energy and NASA scientists with security clearances.

As the proliferation of nuclear weapons barrels on unchecked and a drought of "biblical proportions" grips the United States, Hynek's rhetorical question to Congress whether we can "afford to overlook a potential breakthrough of great significance" is more relevant than ever.

Perhaps more importantly, as Hynek eloquently stated in his congressional testimony, "even if the sole purpose of such a study is to satisfy human curiosity, to probe the unknown and to provide intellectual adventure, then it is in line with what science has always stood for."

Print Citations

CMS: Rennenkampff, Marik von. "UFOs Are an Intriguing Science Problem: Congress Must Act Accordingly." In *The Reference Shelf: UFOs,* edited by Micah L. Issitt, 109-112. Amenia, NY: Grey House Publishing, 2022.

MLA: Rennenkampff, Marik von. "UFOs Are an Intriguing Science Problem: Congress Must Act Accordingly." *The Reference Shelf: UFOs,* edited by Micah L. Issitt, Grey House Publishing, 2022, pp. 109-112.

APA: Rennenkampff, M. von. (2022). UFOs are an intriguing science problem: Congress must act accordingly. In Micah L. Issitt (Ed.), *The reference shelf: UFOs* (pp. 109-112). Amenia, NY: Grey House Publishing.

I'm an Astronomer and I Think Aliens May Be Out There—But UFO Sightings Aren't Persuasive

By Chris Impey
The Conversation, December 4, 2020

If intelligent aliens visit the Earth, it would be one of the most profound events in human history.

Surveys show that nearly half of Americans believe that aliens have visited the Earth, either in the ancient past or recently. That percentage has been increasing. Belief in alien visitation is greater than belief that Bigfoot is a real creature, but less than belief that places can be haunted by spirits.

Scientists dismiss these beliefs as not representing real physical phenomena. They don't deny the existence of intelligent aliens. But they set a high bar for proof that we've been visited by creatures from another star system. As Carl Sagan said, "Extraordinary claims require extraordinary evidence."

I'm a professor of astronomy who has written extensively on the search for life in the universe. I also teach a free online class on astrobiology. Full disclosure: I have not personally seen a UFO.

Unidentified Flying Objects

UFO means unidentified flying object. Nothing more, nothing less.

There's a long history of UFO sightings. Air Force studies of UFOs have been going on since the 1940s. In the United States, "ground zero" for UFOs occurred in 1947 in Roswell, New Mexico. The fact that the Roswell incident was soon explained as the crash landing of a military high-altitude balloon didn't stem a tide of new sightings. The majority of UFOs appear to people in the United States. It's curious that Asia and Africa have so few sightings despite their large populations, and even more surprising that the sightings stop at the Canadian and Mexican borders.

Most UFOs have mundane explanations. Over half can be attributed to meteors, fireballs and the planet Venus. Such bright objects are familiar to astronomers but are often not recognized by members of the public. Reports of visits from UFOs inexplicably peaked about six years ago.

Many people who say they have seen UFOs are either dog walkers or smokers.

Why? Because they're outside the most. Sightings concentrate in evening hours, particularly on Fridays, when many people are relaxing with one or more drinks.

A few people, like former NASA employee James Oberg, have the fortitude to track down and find conventional explanations for decades of UFO sightings. Most astronomers find the hypothesis of alien visits implausible, so they concentrate their energy on the exciting scientific search for life beyond the Earth.

Are We Alone?

While UFOs continue to swirl in the popular culture, scientists are trying to answer the big question that is raised by UFOs: Are we alone?

Astronomers have discovered over 4,000 exoplanets, or planets orbiting other stars, a number that doubles every two years. Some of these exoplanets are considered habitable, since they are close to the Earth's mass and at the right distance from their stars to have water on their surfaces. The nearest of these habitable planets are less than 20 light years away, in our cosmic "back yard." Extrapolating from these

> **Interpreting the Drake Equation in the light of recent exoplanet discoveries makes it very unlikely that we are the only, or the first, advanced civilization.**

results leads to a projection of 300 million habitable worlds in our galaxy. Each of these Earth-like planets is a potential biological experiment, and there have been billions of years since they formed for life to develop and for intelligence and technology to emerge.

Astronomers are very confident there is life beyond the Earth. As astronomer and ace exoplanet-hunter Geoff Marcy, puts it, "The universe is apparently bulging at the seams with the ingredients of biology." There are many steps in the progression from Earths with suitable conditions for life to intelligent aliens hopping from star to star. Astronomers use the Drake Equation to estimate the number of technological alien civilizations in our galaxy. There are many uncertainties in the Drake Equation, but interpreting it in the light of recent exoplanet discoveries makes it very unlikely that we are the only, or the first, advanced civilization.

This confidence has fueled an active search for intelligent life, which has been unsuccessful so far. So researchers have recast the question "Are we alone?" to "Where are they?"

The absence of evidence for intelligent aliens is called the Fermi Paradox. Even if intelligent aliens do exist, there are a number of reasons why we might not have found them and they might not have found us. Scientists do not discount the idea of aliens. But they aren't convinced by the evidence to date because it is unreliable, or because there are so many other more mundane explanations.

Modern Myth and Religion

UFOs are part of the landscape of conspiracy theories, including accounts of abduction by aliens and crop circles created by aliens. I remain skeptical that intelligent beings with vastly superior technology would travel trillion of miles just to press down our wheat.

It's useful to consider UFOs as a cultural phenomenon. Diana Pasulka, a professor at the University of North Carolina, notes that myths and religions are both means for dealing with unimaginable experiences. To my mind, UFOs have become a kind of new American religion.

So no, I don't think belief in UFOs is crazy, because some flying objects are unidentified, and the existence of intelligent aliens is scientifically plausible.

But a study of young adults did find that UFO belief is associated with schizotypal personality, a tendency toward social anxiety, paranoid ideas and transient psychosis. If you believe in UFOs, you might look at what other unconventional beliefs you have.

I'm not signing on to the UFO "religion," so call me an agnostic. I recall the aphorism popularized by Carl Sagan, "It pays to keep an open mind, but not so open your brains fall out."

Print Citations

CMS: Impey, Chris. "I'm an Astronomer and I Think Aliens May Be Out There—but UFO Sightings Aren't Persuasive." In *The Reference Shelf: UFOs,* edited by Micah L. Issitt, 113-115. Amenia, NY: Grey House Publishing, 2022.

MLA: Impey, Chris. "I'm an Astronomer and I Think Aliens May Be Out There—but UFO Sightings Aren't Persuasive." *The Reference Shelf: UFOs,* edited by Micah L. Issitt, Grey House Publishing, 2022, pp. 113-115.

APA: Impey, C. (2022). I'm an astronomer and I think aliens may be out there—but UFO sightings aren't persuasive. In Micah L. Issitt (Ed.), *The reference shelf: UFOs* (pp. 113-115). Amenia, NY: Grey House Publishing.

Scientists Call for Serious Study of "Unidentified Aerial Phenomena"

By Leonard David
Space, October 12, 2020

The U.S. Navy recently admitted that, indeed, strangely behaving objects caught on video by jet pilots over the years are genuine head-scratchers. There are eyewitness accounts not only from pilots but from radar operators and technicians, too.

In August, the Navy established an Unidentified Aerial Phenomena (UAP) Task Force to investigate the nature and origin of these odd sightings and determine if they could potentially pose a threat to U.S. national security.

The recently observed UAPs purportedly have accelerations that range from almost 100 Gs to thousands of Gs—far higher than a human pilot could survive. There's no air disturbance visible. They don't produce sonic booms. These and other oddities have captured the attention of "I told you so, they're here" UFO believers.

But there's also a rising call for this phenomenon to be studied scientifically—even using satellites to be on the lookout for possible future UAP events.

Wanted: High-Quality Evidence

Philippe Ailleris is a project controller at the European Space Agency's Space Research and Technology Center in the Netherlands. He's also the primary force behind the Unidentified Aerospace Phenomena Observations Reporting Scheme, a project to facilitate the collection of UAP reports from both amateur and professional astronomers.

There's a need for the scientific study of UAPs and a requirement to assemble reliable evidence, something that could not be so easily ignored by science, Ailleris told Space.com.

It is necessary to bring scientists objective and high-quality data, Ailleris said. "No one knows where and when a UAP can potentially appear, hence the difficulty of scientific research in this domain."

New Tools

Recent years have seen rapid advances in information and communication technologies—for example, open tools and software, cloud computing and artificial intelligence with machine and deep learning, Ailleris said. These tools offer scientists new possibilities to collect, store, manipulate and transmit data.

Ailleris points to another potent tool. "The location over our heads of satellites is the perfect chance to potentially detect something," he said.

Working in the space sector, it occurred to Ailleris that Earth-observation civilian satellites could be used to search for UAPs. One avenue is tapping into free-of-charge imagery collected by the European Union's Copernicus satellites, an Earth-observing program coordinated and managed by the European Commission in partnership with ESA.

Also, there are more and more Earth-scanning spacecraft being launched to take the pulse of our globe. Such work is no longer limited to major countries or powers, Ailleris said; private actors have also entered the planet-viewing scene.

"This evolution will stimulate forward-thinking ideas across different domains, including controversial topics," Ailleris said. "And why not the UAP research field?"

UAP Expedition

Working with Ailleris to employ satellite imagery to detect and monitor UAPs is Kevin Knuth, a former scientist with NASA's Ames Research Center in California's Silicon Valley. He is now an associate professor of physics at the University at Albany in New York.

"We are looking into using satellites to monitor the region of ocean south of Catalina Island where the 2004 *Nimitz* encounters occurred," Knuth said, referring to UAP sightings reported by pilots and radar operators based aboard the aircraft carrier USS *Nimitz*.

That area will also be the target for a 2021 UAP expedition carried out by Knuth and other researchers. The goal of the outing is "to provide unassailable scientific evidence that UAP objects are real, UAP objects are findable and UAP objects are knowable," according to the website for the project, which is called UAPx.

The UAPx team includes military veterans and physicists, as well as research scientists and trained observers that will use specialized gear to observe any would-be UAP.

> The recently observed UAPs purportedly have accelerations that range from almost 100 Gs to thousands of Gs—far higher than a human pilot could survive.

"We are hoping to detect UAPs, determine their characteristics, flight patterns and any patterns in activity that will allow us to study them more effectively," Knuth told Space.com. "In addition to monitoring a region for UAPs, we are also looking into using satellites to obtain independent confirmation of prominent UAP sightings and to obtain quantifiable information about those UAPs."

Science Problem

"I certainly think that UAP deserve to be studied, just like we would do with any other problem in science," said Jacob Haqq-Misra, an astrobiologist with the Blue Marble Space Institute of Science in Seattle, Washington.

In August, Haqq-Misra helped organize a NASA-sponsored interdisciplinary workshop, called TechnoClimes 2020, that sought to prioritize and guide future theoretical and observational studies of non-radio "technosignatures"—that is, observational manifestations of technology, particularly those that could be detected through astronomical or other means.

Haqq-Misra said his knowledge regarding UAPs stems from the public domain, such as the recently released Navy videos and Department of Defense comments. But otherwise, he has not conducted any of his own investigations into the problem.

"I also remain agnostic as to any particular hypothesis that might explain UAP, at least until we have more data to consider," Haqq-Misra said. "The non-human intelligence hypothesis is a popular one, but I don't necessarily have any indication that it is more probable than any other hypothesis at this point."

"Outlaws" of Physics

Ravi Kopparapu is a planetary scientist at NASA's Goddard Space Flight Center in Greenbelt, Maryland who studies planetary habitability, climate modeling and chemistry in the context of exoplanet atmosphere characterization. He views the UAP/UFO phenomena as a scientifically interesting problem, driven in part by observations that seem to defy the laws of physics.

That said, Kopparapu said he's wary of bringing the term "extraterrestrial" into the conversation. "That's because there is absolutely no concrete evidence that I know of that points to them as being extraterrestrial," he said.

"There's a fundamental problem that we have right now to scientifically study UAP," Kopparapu said. "We do not have proper data collection of this phenomena that can be shared among interested scientists to verify claims and filter out truly unexplainable events."

Also, the entire UAP topic has been much maligned by being associated with ET, Kopparapu added. This association prevents a thorough scientific investigation by the science community, he feels, essentially because of a taboo surrounding ET claims.

"I think people immediately think about 'aliens' when they hear UFOs/UAPs, and I want scientists to not fall for that," Kopparapu said. "Be strictly agnostic and don't let preconceived ideas cloud judgments. Have an open mind. Consider this as a science problem. If it turns out these have mundane explanations, so be it."

Kopparapu and like-minded colleagues are proposing a completely unbiased, agnostic approach to study UAP, he said: "Let the data lead us to what they are."

Print Citations

CMS: David, Leonard. "Scientists Call for Serious Study of 'Unidentified Aerial Phenomena.'" In *The Reference Shelf: UFOs,* edited by Micah L. Issitt, 116-119. Amenia, NY: Grey House Publishing, 2022.

MLA: David, Leonard. "Scientists Call for Serious Study of 'Unidentified Aerial Phenomena.'" *The Reference Shelf: UFOs,* edited by Micah L. Issitt, Grey House Publishing, 2022, pp. 116-119.

APA: David, L. (2022). Scientists call for serious study of "unidentified aerial phenomena." In Micah L. Issitt (Ed.), *The reference shelf: UFOs* (pp. 116-119). Amenia, NY: Grey House Publishing.

Harvard-Led Team to Search Cosmos for Extraterrestrial Space Tech and UFOs

By Mindy Weisberger
Live Science, July 26, 2021

Are there intelligent extraterrestrial civilizations capable of building technologies that can travel between the stars? An international research project is poised to find out.

The Galileo Project, helmed by a multi-institutional team of scientists led by Avi Loeb, a professor of science in the Department of Astronomy at Harvard University, will seek and investigate evidence that could represent defunct or still-active "extraterrestrial technological civilizations," or ETCs, project representatives said in a statement released on Monday (July 26).

The project will analyze data from astronomical surveys and telescope observations, and design new algorithms using artificial intelligence (AI), in order to identify potential interstellar travelers, alien-built satellites and unidentified aerial phenomena (UAP), according to the statement.

"Science should not reject potential extraterrestrial explanations because of social stigma or cultural preferences that are not conducive to the scientific method of unbiased, empirical inquiry," Loeb said in the statement. "We now must 'dare to look through new telescopes,' both literally and figuratively."

Loeb, who is also director of the Institute for Theory and Computation at the Harvard-Smithsonian Center for Astrophysics, has previously suggested that the oddball cosmic object 'Oumuamua—which passed by Earth in 2017 and was widely identified as a comet or asteroid—was an example of alien tech. 'Oumuamua was visible only briefly before it continued on its journey to distant stars, and its flattened, cigarlike shape and erratic motion stymied many astrophysicists; Loeb was one of several scientists who proposed that the object could be a type of spacefaring equipment made by extraterrestrials, *Live Science* previously reported.

"We can only speculate whether 'Oumuamua may be explained by never-seen-before natural explanations, or by stretching our imagination to 'Oumuamua perhaps being an extraterrestrial technological object, similar to a very thin light sail or communications dish, which would fit the astronomical data rather well," Loeb said.

'Oumuamua was our solar system's first interstellar visitor (that we know of, at least), but that doesn't mean it'll be the last, and one of the Galileo Project's research branches will focus on developing strategies for finding and tracking such objects, from space and from ground-based telescopes. Other

> **Science should not reject potential extraterrestrial explanations because of social stigma or cultural preferences.**

project research areas will include searching for small ETC satellites that may be observing Earth, and analysis of UAP sightings.

UAPs—also known as unidentified flying objects, or UFOs—are of particular interest now, following the recent release of an unclassified report by the Pentagon describing UAP sightings by members of the military, Loeb said. Of the 144 UAP sightings between 2004 and 2021 that were documented in the report, just one was identified with "high confidence"—as a deflating balloon. The rest remain unexplained, *Live Science* reported.

"Rigorously Validated" Evidence

The Galileo Project, not to be confused with Rice University's Galileo Project (an online resource for information on Galileo Galilei's life and work) likewise takes its name from the pioneering Italian astronomer, who lived from 1564 to 1642. Galileo used telescopes of his own design to observe celestial objects, leading to astonishing discoveries such as lunar craters, Saturn's rings and the four moons of Jupiter, according to a biography by *Live Science* sister site Space.com.

Galileo's observations and research also confirmed the then-controversial hypothesis of 16th-century astronomer Nicolaus Copernicus: that Earth—and all the solar system's planets—orbited the sun, rather than everything rotating around Earth. Should the Galileo Project discover "rigorously validated scientific evidence of extraterrestrial technology," the impacts would reshape scientists' perception of the cosmos, much as Galileo's discoveries did centuries ago, project representatives wrote in the statement.

Whether or not the Galileo Project will definitively settle the question about intelligent extraterrestrials' existence (and their purported technological prowess) remains to be seen. But actively searching for such physical evidence greatly improves the chances of finding the first examples of alien tech, according to the statement.

As the project's namesake Galileo wrote in "Dialogue Concerning the Two Chief World Systems" in 1632: "All truths are easy to understand once they are discovered—the point is to discover them."

Print Citations

CMS: Weisberger, Mindy. "Harvard-Led Team to Search Cosmos for Extraterrestrial Space Tech and UFOs." In *The Reference Shelf: UFOs,* edited by Micah L. Issitt, 120-122. Amenia, NY: Grey House Publishing, 2022.

MLA: Weisberger, Mindy. "Harvard-Led Team to Search Cosmos for Extraterrestrial Space

Tech and UFOs." *The Reference Shelf: UFOs,* edited by Micah L. Issitt, Grey House Publishing, 2022, pp. 120-122.

APA: Weisberger, M. (2022). Harvard-led team to search cosmos for extraterrestrial space tech and UFOs. In Micah L. Issitt (Ed.), *The reference shelf: UFOs* (pp. 120-122). Amenia, NY: Grey House Publishing.

Pentagon Report Isn't the End of the Search for UFOs: Scientists Say the Right Technology Could Lead to More Answers

By Aparna Nathan

Philadelphia Inquirer, July 1, 2021

After 10 months of investigation, the Pentagon still doesn't know if extraterrestrials are flying overhead.

In a long-awaited report released last week investigating 144 unidentified aerial phenomena, or UAPs, spotted between 2004 and 2021, they were able to explain only a single event: likely a balloon.

These sightings were reported by military pilots detecting inexplicable anomalies with aircraft cameras, which showed distant orbs hovering and appearing to dart through the sky.

Yet even with military-grade sensors, the report shows no evidence of extraterrestrials, even if some of the objects appeared to move with unusual speed and agility. Instead, the task force came up with alternate explanations, including airborne clutter, natural atmospheric phenomena, and military or industrial technology. Separately, the report acknowledges that "some UAP may be attributable to sensor anomalies."

But scientists who specialize in studying the skies think there are more answers to be found.

"Just because we haven't necessarily converged on what the explanation is, the base assumption is that it's probably something we can explain if we have enough data," said Melanie Good, a lecturer in physics and astronomy at the University of Pittsburgh.

Mark Miller, a professor of atmospheric science at Rutgers University, isn't surprised that preliminary results are inconclusive. He has spent his career pointing cameras at the skies to study complex patterns of clouds and energy in the atmosphere, so he knows just how hard it can be.

"We're always seeing new things and it always takes a while to reconcile what we're seeing when we deploy these more advanced sensors," he said. "In a sense, we expect the unexpected."

Moreover, these particular sensors might not be up to the task of finding UAPs.

"Military equipment is not designed to provide the best scientific data," said

Avi Loeb, a professor of science at Harvard University who studies astrophysics. "It's designed to do something useful for the military"—to quickly detect and report a potential threat.

> **The kind of equipment required to collect high-quality data on UAPs would be more than what a small fighter jet could accommodate.**

Miller added that the kind of equipment required to collect high-quality data on UAPs would be more than what a small fighter jet needs or could accommodate.

A variety of high-tech sensors from military aircraft collected the UAP data used in the investigation, but each sensor still has its quirks. Infrared, for example, detects heat energy. Planes use forward-looking infrared (FLIR) to see through fog or smoke that obscures their vision. A FLIR camera on a naval plane recorded a video of a heat-emitting orb in 2004, and another video was captured in 2015.

Radar, on the other hand, works by sending out radio waves and measuring how much is reflected back. In planes, its purpose is to detect the position and speed of hazards in the surrounding airspace; radar is what alerted the pilots in 2004 to investigate the UAP.

Astrophysicists, meteorologists, and atmospheric scientists use similar sensors for their own research and are well-versed in all the ways they can go wrong. Miller says there's especially high risk of false readings with new sensor technology, which has proven true for past UFO sightings.

"I can't tell you the number of occasions in the past when we've deployed a new sensor, and then discovered artifacts over time," Miller said. In particular, these unexpected blips can arise from the complex calculations that computers have to do to create an image—but to unravel that, scientists would need the raw data from the sensors, not just the final image, he said.

Optical illusions can also occur because of the sensor's position, Good said. One example, the bokeh effect, occurs when the opening in the camera reshapes out-of-focus light, Good said. Objects can also appear to have unusual velocity if the viewer misjudges their distance.

And the biggest variable of all: the sky. Even if it seems like a void, the sky is actually chock full of water droplets and ice crystals forming clouds, birds and bugs, balloons, and other debris, not to mention the energy and heat fluctuations that create phenomena like the Northern Lights, said Drew Anderson, a meteorologist at WFMZ-TV 69 News and adjunct professor at West Chester University.

The report acknowledges this, specifying that natural atmospheric phenomena such as ice crystals, moisture, or heat could account for part of the UAP sightings. Sensors depend on waves traveling through the air to signal that an object exists. But when these waves encounter other particles in the air, like ice crystals, water droplets—or even pollen and pollution—the particles can disrupt the wave's path back to the sensor in both predictable and unpredictable ways. Pockets of heat or other energy building up in the atmosphere may also show up on IR.

That's why it can be hard to detect objects accurately in unfamiliar places, Miller said. He pointed to one UAP sighting in California in July, a time when the clouds around California are particularly low and can appear denser based on pollution.

"You're at the mercy of the atmosphere," Miller said.

However, the fact that more than half the sightings were detected on multiple sensors that use different detection methods may signal that it's not an error, Loeb said.

More than half of Americans surveyed by Pew Research Center think military reports of UAPs are probably evidence of life on other planets, and 87% don't see UAPs as a major threat.

So, what would it take to study UAPs in earnest? For starters, collaborative science and funding, Loeb said.

They'd also need the right technology. Wide-field cameras—like the one on the Hubble Space Telescope—could help scientists look for UAPs in larger sections of the sky. A network of multiple high-end research sensors would need to be optimized to measure the right kinds of heat, movement, and size. They would also need more powerful computers for storing, processing, and sharing the data.

UAP research "should move to the realm of science where we will collect more evidence in an open fashion," Loeb said. "The sky is not classified."

Print Citations

CMS: Nathan, Aparna. "Pentagon Report Isn't the End of the Search for UFOs: Scientists Say the Right Technology Could Lead to More Answers." In *The Reference Shelf: UFOs,* edited by Micah L. Issitt, 123-125. Amenia, NY: Grey House Publishing, 2022.

MLA: Nathan, Aparna. "Pentagon Report Isn't the End of the Search for UFOs: Scientists Say the Right Technology Could Lead to More Answers." *The Reference Shelf: UFOs,* edited by Micah L. Issitt, Grey House Publishing, 2022, pp. 123-125.

APA: Nathan, A. (2022). Pentagon report isn't the end of the search for UFOs: Scientists say the right technology could lead to more answers. In Micah L. Issitt (Ed.), *The reference shelf: UFOs* (pp. 123-125). Amenia, NY: Grey House Publishing.

5
The View from Above

Alien abduction became popular after the 1961 alleged abduction of Betty and Barney Hill made national headlines. Images of alien encounters in the woods became standard in the popular imagination.

The Mystery of Alien Abduction

The idea of visiting aliens abducting humans or animals for experimental (or other) purposes has become a common and familiar aspect of UFO lore and fiction. From science fiction classics like *Close Encounters of the Third Kind* (1977) to children's films like *Flight of the Navigator* (1986) to psychological dramas like *Fire in the Sky* (1993), alien abduction has become a key subgenre in the field of speculative extraterrestrial fiction. Some may be drawn to the idea of alien abduction out of curiosity about the unknown and a desire to experience otherworldly phenomena but, in many cases, the alien abduction trope appears to express the similar kinds of fears of the unknown that also motivate interest in ghosts and supernatural creatures.

While alien abductions make for an interesting theme in fantasy fiction, there are many Americans who believe that alien abductions actually occur. A 2017 20th Century Fox survey found that around 18 to 20 percent of Americans believe that aliens have abducted humans at some point in the past. This was out of a total of 39 percent of respondents who believed that aliens had visited Earth before (with a full 47 percent believing that aliens exist at all).[1] Belief in actual alien abduction has been fueled by first-person accounts from people who claim either to have been abducted themselves or to have witnessed an abduction. Reports from those who claim to have been abductees tend to share certain themes and even more specific depictions of alien features and technology that has been interpreted, by believers, as evidence that aliens really are taking people, for still unknown purposes.

Anatomy of a Myth

No one knows when the idea of extraterrestrial visitors first arose or when the first person claimed to have been abducted, but abduction stories didn't really become a common part of the alien genre until the 1960s, when an unassuming couple named Betty and Barney Hill became victims of the first famous abduction event in American history.

In 1961, the Hills were driving through New Hampshire's White Mountains while on vacation when they claimed they realized they were being followed by a brightly glowing flying object. Neither remembered what happened next, but several hours later they seemed to awaken with dirty and slightly damaged clothes, evidence of some minor physical trauma, watches that had mysteriously stopped working, and no memory of the previous two hours.

After months of sleeplessness and strange dreams, the couple sought help and, under the influence of hypnosis, a strange picture began to emerge. Betty and Barney described having been pursued by a strange, disc-shaped ship that eventually landed in front of them. The ship opened and a group of short gray aliens emerged. The aliens appeared friendly and guided the two back into the ship where they were separated and placed onto examination tables. The aliens then performed a number of medical tests, including collecting skin samples, using various probes, and even utilizing a large needle to sample material from Betty Hill's reproductive system. After some additional friendly conversation, the aliens erased the couple's memories and returned them to their vehicle.

When the stories about Betty and Barney's experiences began to circulate, the couple became minor celebrities. They were invited on talk shows, interviewed by numerous journalists, and were even the subjects of a full-fledged US Air Force investigation. Even decades after, it remains uncertain what exactly happened that night on the road through New Hampshire, but Betty and Barney's story spread far and wide, and before long other people started coming forward with similar stories. Betty and Barney became the most famous abductees in what became one of the most familiar subgenres in American extraterrestrial legend.[2]

Betty and Barney's story captivated Americans when articles about their alleged encounter began to emerge in 1965. The book that they wrote became a bestseller and a movie based on their claims was made starring James Earl Jones. While the Hills weren't the first to report being abducted, they were the first to claim that they'd been taken as experimental subjects. Sociologist Christopher Bader, of Chapman University in California, explained in a 1995 study of abduction stories how the Hills story changed the entire dialogue on UFOs across the country. Prior to media coverage of the Hills, there was no standardized depiction of aliens among those who claimed to have seen them. After the Hills, however, more and more of the stories involving abduction and other encounters involved what UFO aficionados came to call "the grays," short-bodied gray aliens with large heads and huge almond-shaped dark eyes. Similar aliens appeared on the X-Files television series and in the film Close Encounters of the Third Kind, which drew much of its inspiration from stories like the Hills'.

Bader traced the popularity of this kind of alien design to the media attention afforded to the Hills after their reported encounter. In the decades that followed, hundreds of other Americans claimed to be abducted and told stories similar to the one revealed by the Hills through hypnosis, including saucer-shaped metal ships with bright white and red lights and short, gray aliens who were friendly but subjected captives to scientific medical-style experiments. These stories were so convincing that even some respected scientists came to express their belief in abductions, most notably John E. Mack, a Harvard psychiatrist who founded the Program for Extraordinary Experience Research (PEER), which sought to investigate reports of abductions from around the world. In his 1995 book Abduction, Mack explained why he had come to believe that abductions were real.[3]

What Happened in New Hampshire?

The fact that alleged abductees tend to describe the events of their abductions in similar ways has been interpreted, by some, as evidence that abductions have actually occurred, but there are many ways to interpret the evidence, or lack thereof. The similarities between reports might also be interpreted as reason to be skeptical of alien abduction stories because each abduction story that gains popularity might also inspire imaginative fantasies in others. Psychologist Richard McNally studied alien abduction stories and came to believe that the same psychological mechanisms involved in reports of abduction might also explain perceptions of visions from past lives and other kinds of fantastic, out-of-body experiences.

In his 2012 article, "Explaining 'Memories' of Space Alien Abduction and Past Lives: An Experimental Psychopathology Approach," McNally and students, "used methods of experimental psychopathology to explain why seemingly sincere, non-psychotic people claim to have memories of being abducted by space aliens or memories from past lives." McNally and colleagues determined that the most likely explanation was that abductees were experiencing "sleep paralysis," a condition in which an individual has a sense of being conscious but is unable to move.[4] The condition is related to the chemicals that are exuded by the brain to prevent accidental movement and injury during sleep but often manifest in feelings of extreme dread or fear. People who have sleep paralysis also commonly report being visited by ghosts or demons, which is one of the ways that the half-waking state can manifest in the mind of a person suffering from this type of physical condition. When the individual begins to wake up, they may also experience what are known as "hypnopompic hallucinations," in which a person might see, feel, or see things that are not actually there as their brain transitions between a sleeping and waking state.[5]

McNally and other psychologists have suggested that the combination of sleep paralysis and hypnopompic hallucination is sufficient to describe the stories of alien abduction, but this does not explain why the experiences of abductees are so similar. This might be explained by the fact that alleged abductees have unconsciously incorporated the common mythology and imagery of UFO and alien myth into their subconscious minds, with these visions manifesting as their brains try to make sense of strange sensations and visions occurring in a half-conscious state.

There is another interesting feature to McNally's research and other studies of abductee reports, which is that researchers have found that abductees demonstrate a high degree of what is sometimes called "magical thinking," in comparison to the population as a whole. In the McNally study, for instance, the researchers found that 70 percent of abductees also believed in tarot card readings, in comparison to only 8 percent in the general population. Similarly, individuals who claimed to have been abducted showed a tendency to believe in other nonphysical phenomenon for which there is no clear evidence, like alternative herbal medicines, telepathy, and ghosts. It appears then that abductees tend to be people who are already primed to embrace phenomenon without necessarily depending on direct evidence, and this may increase the likelihood that these same people would interpret unusual experiences to some larger alleged phenomenon.

Further, studies of abduction often reveal that individuals who claim to have been abducted embrace their abduction as an important part of their personality and appear highly skeptical or resistant to any other explanation of what they have experienced. One common theme in abduction stories is the idea that aliens would harvest sperm or eggs in order to potentially repopulate the species, and a number of alleged abductees express pride that they were "special" enough to be of interest to aliens and that their genes might be preserved in whatever genetic breeding experiments the aliens might be conducting. Research indicates, therefore, that individuals who believe they have been abducted also demonstrate a high degree of interest in preserving their abduction experience as a signifier of special identity or significance on a broader spiritual (or in this case cosmic) sense.

Part of the reason that Betty and Barney Hill's abduction story gained so much popularity was because the couple were described as intelligent, otherwise sober, people who did not believe in UFOs prior to their experience. Researchers who studied them and interviewed them made note of their reasonable behavior and lack of any evidence of mental illness. Some have suggested, however, that there might have been subtle psychological reasons that the couple would have embraced such an incredible explanation for what they experienced. Being an interracial couple living in an area in which such couples were vanishingly rare, and in the midst of the civil rights movement, Betty and Barney's celebrity may have been, in part, a reflection of their shared stress and experiences. Some have noted that it is interesting that Betty and Barney's alien abductors appeared to them with gray skin, with gray being a mix of white and black, not unlike the couple's unique experience of their own world, in which their differences from the other couples they would have seen and known, meant that they were aliens in another sense.

Works Used

Bader, Chris D. "The UFO Contact Movement from the 1950s to the Present." *Studies in Popular Culture*. Vol. 17, No. 2. Apr. 1995.

Davis, Kathleen. "Everything You Need to Know About Sleep Paralysis." *Medical News Today*. May 24, 2017. Retrieved from https://www.medicalnewstoday.com/articles/295039.

McNally, Richard J. "Explaining 'Memories' of Space Alien Abduction and Past Lives: An Experimental Psychopathology Approach." *Journal of Experimental Psychopathology*. Vol. 3, No. 1, 2012.

Rojas, Alejandro. "New Survey Shows Nearly Half of Americans Believe in Aliens." *Huffpost*. Aug. 2, 2017. Retrieved from https://www.huffpost.com/entry/new-survey-shows-nearly-half-of-americans-believe-in_b_59824c11e4b-03d0624b0abe4.

Weiss, Josh. "New Docu-Series Explores How Betty and Barney Hill Changed UFO Culture with Their Famous Story of Alien Abduction." *Syfy*. Aug. 25, 2021. Retrieved from https://www.syfy.com/syfy-wire/betty-barney-hill-ufo-showtime.

Notes

1. Rojas, "New Survey Shows Nearly Half of Americans Believe in Aliens."
2. Weiss, "New Docu-Series Explores How Betty and Barney Hill Changed UFO Culture With Their Famous Story of Alien Abduction."
3. Bader, "The UFO Contact Movement from the 1950s to the Present."

4. Davis, "Everything You Need to Know About Sleep Paralysis."
5. McNally, "Explaining 'Memories' of Space Alien Abduction and Past Lives: An Experimental Psychopathology Approach."

"Alien Abduction" Stories May Come from Lucid Dreaming, Study Hints

By Mindy Weisberger
Live Science, July 19, 2021

Lucid dreaming, in which people are partially aware and can control their dreams during sleep, could explain so-called alien abduction stories, a study suggests.

Claims of such abductions date to the 19th century; the circumstances of the kidnappings often sound dreamlike and trigger feelings of terror and paralysis. Certain dream states are also known to produce such feelings, leading Russian researchers to wonder if dream experiments could provide clues about alleged extraterrestrial experiences. The scientists prompted lucid dreamers to dream about encounters with aliens or unidentified flying objects (UFOs), and found that a number of sleepers reported dreams that resembled actual descriptions of alleged alien abductions.

During lucid dreams, sleepers are aware they are dreaming and can then use that awareness to manipulate what happens in the dream. About 55% of people experience lucid dreaming once or more in their lifetimes, and 23% have lucid dreams at least once a month, according to a 2016 study in the journal *Consciousness and Cognition* that analyzed five decades' worth of sleep research.

Recently, researchers with the Phase Research Center (PRC), a private facility in Moscow that researches lucid dreaming, conducted experiments with 152 adults who self-identified as lucid dreamers, instructing them to "find or summon aliens or UFOs" during a lucid dream, the scientists reported July 2 in the *International Journal of Dream Research*.

The researchers found that 114 of the participants reported dreaming about having some type of successful interaction with an extraterrestrial. Of those, about 61% described meeting "aliens" that resembled extraterrestrials from science-fiction novels and films, while 19% met aliens that "looked like ordinary people," according to the study.

Little Blue Men

One female participant spoke of seeing "little men" with blue skin, oversize heads "and huge, bulging eyes," the study authors reported. When the aliens invited her onto their spaceship, "I was blinded by a very bright light, like from a searchlight," she said. "My vision was gone, and I felt dizzy and light."

Another participant said that he dreamed he was lying in his bed when he felt as though he

> **Feelings of paralysis, fear and helplessness in vivid dreams can be so powerful that they blur the line between dreams and reality.**

were being "dragged somewhere," ending up in a room with a white silhouette that reached into his chest and started "doing something inside with tools," the researchers wrote.

Conversations with dream aliens took place in 26% of the encounters, and 12% of the participants spoke with aliens in their dreams and interacted with them physically. UFOs showed up in 28% of the meetings, and 10% of the dreamers who saw UFOs described being brought inside an extraterrestrial spacecraft.

Of those who described their encounters as "realistic," 24% also experienced sleep paralysis and intense fear. Such emotions often accompany reports of supposed alien abductions, and though individuals who describe being kidnapped by aliens might truly believe that what they experienced was real, these people were likely experiencing an extraterrestrial meeting while in a lucid dream, the study authors reported.

Feelings of paralysis, fear and helplessness in vivid dreams can be so powerful that they blur the line between dreams and reality, so it's no wonder that people who may have unknowingly been dreaming instead insist that they actually met with aliens who stole them away and transported them to UFOs, said PRC head researcher and founder Michael Raduga.

For these unknowing dreamers, "abductions are real," Raduga told *Live Science* in an email. "They just don't know how to explain it."

Print Citations

CMS: Weisberger, Mindy. "'Alien Abduction' Stories May Come from Lucid Dreaming, Study Hints." In *The Reference Shelf: UFOs,* edited by Micah L. Issitt, 135-136. Amenia, NY: Grey House Publishing, 2022.

MLA: Weisberger, Mindy. "'Alien Abduction' Stories May Come from Lucid Dreaming, Study Hints." *The Reference Shelf: UFOs,* edited by Micah L. Issitt, Grey House Publishing, 2022, pp. 135-136.

APA: Weisberger, M. (2022). "Alien abduction" stories may come from lucid dreaming, study hints. In Micah L. Issitt (Ed.), *The reference shelf: UFOs* (pp. 135-136). Amenia, NY: Grey House Publishing.

Ghouls and Alien Abduction? You Just Might Have Sleep Paralysis!

By Simon Spichak
Medium, July 31, 2021

It's the middle of the night, it feels like 2 or 3 am. The wind howls outside, violently shaking my window. As always, my eyes are wide open, I am paralyzed and I wait. Yet every time the Shadow Man visits, I am terrified again. I still try to scream and try to will the muscles in my legs to work again so I can run. The figure looms over my bed for what seems to be an eternity, its shadowy hands extending towards my chest. All I can do is wait, wait for it all to be over. I feel it pressing down on my chest. I feel like I'm suffocating but in the back of my mind, I know none of this can be real.

No, this is not an excerpt from a horror novel or a creative writing exercise. Many people around the world report these otherworldly, creepy manifestations and visitations. This phenomenon is present in almost every culture, inspiring much of our horror mythos. Despite differences across cultures, there are common trends across many of these visitations: difficulty breathing, feeling suffocated, and being paralyzed in bed. These waking nightmares are symptomatic of *sleep paralysis*. Our brain shuts off parts of our body while we're asleep and dreaming. However, occasionally something will go awry. It's common for this to happen to us once or twice throughout the course of our lifetime. However, for an unfortunate few, sleep paralysis becomes an almost nightly occurrence.

There are many documentaries featuring accounts of sleep paralysis. I've linked the trailer for *The Nightmare* (2015) that features the common manifestation of the Shadow Man.

This phenomenon is present in almost every culture, inspiring much of our horror mythos. Despite differences across cultures, there are common trends across many of these visitations: difficulty breathing, feeling suffocated and being paralyzed in bed.

How Does Sleep Paralysis Occur?

It is estimated that sleep paralysis happens at least once for up to 2 in 5 people! For most individuals, this only happens once or twice during their life. Rather than being in an unconscious sleeping state during the REM-phase, they are conscious while dreaming. They are paralyzed and often experience what they describe as intruders in their bedroom, alien abductions and a variety of other horrifying nightmares.

There are several stages of sleep that our brain cycles through while we rest. One of these cycles is called the rapid-eye-movement (REM) stage of sleep. It's in this phase that we dream every night. It first occurs 90 minutes after we fall asleep, lasting about 10 minutes. The brain first cycles through four stages of non-REM sleep.

Once we enter REM-sleep, our eyes move quickly in many different directions while the rest of our body is kept still. The brain sends signals to the rest of the body preventing any thrashing or movement so that we don't injure ourselves by acting out our dreams. This stage is also characterized by higher levels of brain activity, resulting in vivid dreams. Throughout the night, we cycle through non-REM and REM sleep, which each subsequent REM cycle lasting longer and longer. Typically, the last REM phase of the night can last an hour.

Neuroscientists Dr. Patricia Brooks and Dr. John H. Peever discovered that two neurotransmitters are responsible for making sure we don't move in REM sleep. These two neurotransmitters are called gamma-amino-butyric acid (GABA) and glycine.

Each of these neurotransmitters is like a key, that is able to turn and activate specific locks within the brain. These regions are located in the **brainstem**, called the pons and the medulla. These locks are receptors that tell regions of the brain to slow their firing. Since the parts of the brain with these lock-receptors are involved in muscle control, it ensures our limbs remain still.

There are other important brain regions involved during REM sleep.

- **Suprachiasmatic Nucleus of the Hypothalamus:** This region of the brain contains light-sensitive cells. They act as pacemakers during our sleep. This includes coordinating other areas of our brain and ensuring that other tissues within the body adapt accordingly.

- **Amygdala:** This part of the brain adds an emotional component to our brain.

- **Thalamus:** This part of the brain relays information from our senses during wakefulness. While we're in non-REM stages of sleep, this part of the brain is shut off, tuning out environmental stimuli. However, once we enter the REM stage, this area begins firing to coordinate the sound, visuals, and other senses within our dreams. The occipital lobe in our cerebral cortex for example, responsible for our visual perception, generates vivid visuals in our dreams.

This stage of sleep is fascinating. Parts of our brain are awake enough to dream, but other parts are suppressed just enough to keep us from waking.

It is estimated that sleep paralysis happens at least once for up to 2 in 5 people! For most individuals, this only happens once or twice during their life. Rather than being in an unconscious sleeping state during the REM-phase, they are conscious while dreaming. They are paralyzed and often experience what they describe as intruders in their bedroom, alien abductions and a variety of other horrifying nightmares.

Nobody knows what causes sleep paralysis, though it's linked to several other disorders: including generalized anxiety disorder, post-traumatic stress disorder, panic dis-

> **Despite differences across cultures, there are common trends across many of these visitations: difficulty breathing, feeling suffocated and being paralyzed in bed.**

orders and other sleep disturbances. Some individuals afflicted by sleep paralysis even report learning to enjoy the experiences, like an immersive horror show.

Goblins, Ghosts, Grey-Aliens, and Goons

While the neurobiology of sleep is of utmost importance to learn more about sleep paralysis, our culture also plays an important role. The brain incorporates previous information to make the most sense of it. When it comes to sleep paralysis, the current cultural zeitgeist greatly influences which intruders visit us in the middle of the night. Across different times and different countries, people experience this very same phenomenon differently.

Hundreds of years ago, Americans and Canadians believed that beings were draining their life energy at night, attributing sleep paralysis to vampires or witches. In recent decades, this was replaced by alien abductions and shadow people. In Thailand, people report being enveloped by a ghost, calling the experience *phĭ̆ am*. In Iran, there is a similar experience called *Kabus* described as a heavy presence sitting on the chest, suffocating you.

Sleep paralysis is even described in Herman Melville's 1851 novel, *Moby Dick*:

My arm hung over the counterpane, and the nameless, unimaginable silent form or phantom, to which the hand belonged, seemed closely seated by my bedside. For what seemed ages piled on ages, I lay there, frozen with the most awful fears, not daring to drag away my hand; yet ever thinking that if I could but stir it one single inch, the horrid spell would be broken.

Broad cultural differences and distances separate us from people in other countries. Despite these large fundamental differences, we still experience the same phenomena when we sleep. Even though cultural manifestations differ, there are so many uncanny similarities.

Human psychology is fundamentally similar, no matter what time or place you've been born into. Our brain confabulates extravagant explanations, based on previous cultural information to understand ourselves the world around us. This truly weird phenomenon is humbling—it can happen to anyone, anywhere no matter how rich or smart you are. It reinforces the necessity of understanding other cultural experiences in order to better understand the biology of sleep paralysis.

Print Citations

CMS: Spichak, Simon. "Ghouls and Alien Abduction? You Just Might Have Sleep Paralysis!" In *The Reference Shelf: UFOs,* edited by Micah L. Issitt, 137-140. Amenia, NY: Grey House Publishing, 2022.

MLA: Spichak, Simon. "Ghouls and Alien Abduction? You Just Might Have Sleep Paralysis!" *The Reference Shelf: UFOs,* edited by Micah L. Issitt, Grey House Publishing, 2022, pp. 137-140.

APA: Spichak, S. (2022). Ghouls and alien abduction? You just might have sleep paralysis! In Micah L. Issitt (Ed.), *The reference shelf: UFOs* (pp. 137-140). Amenia, NY: Grey House Publishing.

Some Scientific Explanations for Alien Abduction That Aren't So Out of This World

By Ken Drinkwater and Neil Dagnall
The Conversation, January 27, 2017

Accounts of mysterious flashing lights in the sky, spacecrafts and encounters with "real" aliens reflect high levels of public interest in UFOs and the belief that there is "something out there". However, many psychologists are less convinced, and think they can provide more down-to-earth, scientific explanations.

Belief in aliens has increased steadily since the birth of modern alien research in the 1940s and 1950s, following the news surrounding a classified US military project at Roswell Air Force Base, New Mexico. Surveys in Western cultures estimated belief in aliens to be as high as 50% in 2015. And despite the fact that it is considered rare, a significant number of people also believe they have experienced alien abduction.

Present day awareness of alien abduction dates to the 1961 case of Betty and Barney Hill, who witnessed odd lights and experienced "missing time" and "lost memories" while driving. The reported consequences of abduction are often loss of memory, missing time, and problems such as sickness, sleepwalking, nightmares and psychological trauma. Following their experience, Betty and Barney experienced psychological problems and subsequently sought therapy.

Although the accuracy of the numbers is questioned, a poll by the Roper Center for Public Opinion Research conducted 30 years after this account said that around 3.7m Americans believed that they too had experienced alien abduction.

Sceptics argue that alien-related encounters are merely hoaxes created for financial gain or social advantage. Perhaps Roswell is the most famous example. Initial reports from the 1940s left sufficient gaps of explanation for Ray Santilli to release in 1995 what he claimed was film footage showing an alien autopsy from the time, further confusing the issue. He later admitted it was a hoax. The incident sparked controversy and prompted claims that an alien craft had crash-landed in the New Mexico desert and that US authorities were involved in a cover-up.

The theory that alien abductions are hoaxes may be true in a few cases, but there is no reason to assume that the majority of "experiencers" are frauds. In fact, psychologists have come up with a number of plausible, scientific explanations for people's supposed alien encounters.

Personality Traits

One explanation is that when people believe they have had an experience of alien abduction, they have misinterpreted, distorted and conflated real and imagined events. Hence, sceptics of alien encounters explain them away in terms of psychological processes and personality characteristics.

Several studies report that experiencers do not typically differ from non-experiencers on objective psychopathological measures–those that assess psychological well-being and adjustment–and have no history of mental instability. However, one characteristic that is associated with abduction experiences is a proclivity for fantasy.

Mixed evidence supports the theory that fantasy-prone people engage in elaborate imaginings and often confuse fantasy with reality. There are also other psychological explanations, such as dissociation–where an individual's mental processes detach from each other and from reality, often in response to extreme or stressful life events. A tendency towards being fantasy-prone and dissociation has been linked in studies to childhood trauma and hypnotic suggestibility.

Psychologists argue that hypnosis encourages the creation and recall of detailed fantasies. For example, Betty and Barney Hill's account was typical of reported alien encounters: medical examinations or procedures, communication with alien captors, a powerful, mystical feeling, tours of spaceships and journeys to other planets before being returned to the car. And it was under hypnosis that these "missing memories" were "recovered".

It's for these reasons that it's believed alien abduction experiences may arise from a combination of personality characteristics and susceptibility to false memories.

Brain Sensitivity

Studies suggest that neuropsychological theories, particularly sleep paralysis and temporal lobe sensitivity, also could explain claims of alien abduction.

Sleep paralysis is a feeling of being conscious but unable to move, which occurs when a person passes between stages of wakefulness and sleep.

Experiencers' claims share characteristics with sleep paralysis: a sense of being awake, not dreaming, and realistic perceptions of the environment. The inability to move, a feeling of fear or dread, and the sense of another presence–perhaps evil or malevolent–are common symptoms. Also common are a feeling of pressure on the chest and difficulty breathing, and of being held or restricted to a lying position: most sleep paralysis attacks occur while the individual is lying on their back.

Sceptic Michael Shermer once collapsed from sleep deprivation following an 83-hour bike race and his support team rushed to his aid. Shermer was caught in a "waking dream" and so perceived them as aliens from the 1960s television series *The Invaders*. It also explains some ghost sightings, such as the "night hag", often experienced by those who suffer from sleep paralysis.

Temporal lobe sensitivity is a theory that suggests the temporal lobes of some people's brains are more vulnerable to influence from low-level magnetic frequencies. Michael Persinger, a neuroscientist at Laurentian University in Canada, is among those who believes that increased temporal lobe activity can explain paranormal experiences such as alien abduction. His theory is that

> **Alien abduction experiences may arise from a combination of personality characteristics and susceptibility to false memories.**

magnetic fields stimulate the temporal lobes, resulting in hallucinatory experiences similar to those reported by alien abductees.

None of this is to say that many people who believe they have experienced alien abduction are liars, merely that their accounts and experiences can be explained through recourse to theories with a scientific basis. There are many logical, plausible scientific explanations, none of which rely upon the existence of aliens. However, it should also be noted that not all reported alien abduction experiences can be easily explained by any of these scientific theories—and this throws up many more questions.

Print Citations

CMS: Drinkwater, Ken, and Neil Dagnall. "Some Scientific Explanations for Alien Abduction That Aren't So Out of This World." In *The Reference Shelf: UFOs,* edited by Micah L. Issitt, 141-143. Amenia, NY: Grey House Publishing, 2022.

MLA: Drinkwater, Ken, and Neil Dagnall. "Some Scientific Explanations for Alien Abduction That Aren't So Out of This World." *The Reference Shelf: UFOs,* edited by Micah L. Issitt, Grey House Publishing, 2022, pp. 141-143.

APA: Drinkwater, K., & Dagnall, N. (2022). Some scientific explanations for alien abduction that aren't so out of this world. In Micah L. Issitt (Ed.), *The reference shelf: UFOs* (pp. 141-143). Amenia, NY: Grey House Publishing.

Alien Abduction Claims Examined: Signs of Trauma Found

By William J. Cromie
Harvard Gazette, February 20, 2003

Richard McNally doesn't believe people have been abducted by aliens, but he believes he knows why they believe it.

Mark H. says he was abducted by aliens. He clearly remembers awakening one night, unable to move anything but his eyes. He saw flashing lights, heard buzzing sounds, experienced feelings of levitation, and felt electric tingling sensations. Most terrifying were the nonhuman figures he saw by his bed.

Mark believes they were aliens.

Later, he underwent hypnosis to try to recall exactly what had happened to him. Under hypnosis, Mark remembered being whisked through an open window to a large spaceship. He was very frightened when aliens took him into some kind of medical examining room. There he had sex with one of them.

Afterward, the aliens brought him back to Earth and returned him to his bed.

Mark describes the experience as terrifying. But did it really happen?

Some researchers at Harvard University devised an experiment to determine if memories of an abduction by space aliens would provoke the same physiological reactions that occur when other people, such as combat veterans and those who survive deadly car accidents, recall their traumatic experiences.

Richard McNally, a professor of psychology, and his colleagues recruited six women and four men who claimed they had been spirited away by extraterrestrials, some of them more than once. Under hypnosis, seven of the 10 reported having had their sperm or eggs extracted for breeding purposes, or experiencing direct sexual contact with the space aliens.

Each of these people was interviewed by either McNally or Susan Clancy, also a professor of psychology. Each also wrote a script that told the story of his or her abduction. The research team then made audiotapes, spoken in a neutral voice, from the scripts. The abductees listened to these tapes in the laboratory of Scott Orr at the Veteran's Affairs Medical Center in Manchester, N.H. As the tapes played, the researchers recorded their emotional responses using such measures as heart rate and sweat on the palms of their hands.

The same procedure was done with eight people haunted by traumatic experiences unrelated to abduction by aliens.

When the two sets of measurements were compared, the results were striking. Abductees showed surprisingly strong physiological reactions to the tapes of their alien encounters. Their reactions were as great or greater than those of individuals who cannot shake memories of combat, sexual abuse, and other punishing events.

McNally announced these findings on Feb. 16 at a meeting of the American Association for the Advancement of Science in Denver. "The results underscore the power of emotional belief," he noted. "People who sincerely believe they have been abducted by aliens show patterns of emotional and physiological response to these 'memories' that are strikingly similar to those of people who have been genuinely traumatized by combat or similar events."

Dreaming with Their Eyes Wide Open

Neither McNally nor the other Harvard researchers ever considered the possibility that people in the study, or anybody else, was ever abducted by space aliens. But, if not, what produced their lasting vivid memories?

The researchers tie such abduction stories to a phenomenon they call "dreaming with your eyes wide open." The episodes occur just as people awaken from a dream. Dreams include full-body paralysis, a nice adaptation that prevents people from jumping out of bed to escape their demons, or otherwise making moves in a dream that could injure them in reality. The sleeper awakens from a dream before the paralysis goes away, and experiences hallucinations like seeing flashing lights and some kinds of living things lurking around the bed.

Sleep paralysis is common and no more indicative of mental illness than a hiccup, the researchers point out. But when the hallucination and paralysis occur together, many people find the combination frightening, and they attempt to find a meaning in it.

Some individuals consult psychiatrists or psychologists who hypnotize them to recover presumably repressed memories that lie behind the strange

> When the hallucination and paralysis occur together, many people find the combination frightening, and they attempt to find a meaning in it.

events. During such sessions, a person may recover false memories of being transported up into spacecraft where they were subjected to medical and sexual experiments.

Psychological interviews and tests conducted on the abductees reveal little evidence of mental illness, but they enjoy a rich fantasy life. When they listen to music or watch movies they often imagine they are somewhere else or part of the movie plot. The typical abductee, notes McNally, "has a longstanding interest in 'New Age' practices and beliefs such as reincarnation, astral projection, mental telepathy, alternative healing practices, energy therapies, and astrology."

He and his colleagues conclude, "a combination of pre-existing New Age beliefs, episodes of sleep paralysis, accompanied by hallucinations and hypnotic memory recovery may foster beliefs and memories that one has been abducted by space aliens."

Ghost, Hags, and Incubi

Such combinations give rise to a variety of interpretations across cultures and throughout history, McNally points out. Not everyone who has been scared by this experience imagines they have been abducted by aliens.

A hallucination upon awakening from a dream might be interpreted as a visit from a ghost or Satan. In Newfoundland, people have encounters with the "Old Hag," a witch who gets on your bed with you. Hundreds of years ago in Europe, people feared the incubus, an evil spirit that lies on people while they sleep, or the succubus, a demon who assumes a female form and has sex with men in their sleep.

Abductees react emotionally like people who have real memories of combat, abuse, and near-death encounters, but most of them are glad they had contact with extraterrestrials. Some say they feel pleased to have been chosen to take part in hybrid breeding programs. Most of them, says McNally, "ultimately interpret their experience as spiritually transforming."

Print Citations

CMS: Cromie, William J. "Alien Abduction Claims Examined: Signs of Trauma Found." In *The Reference Shelf: UFOs,* edited by Micah L. Issitt, 144-146. Amenia, NY: Grey House Publishing, 2022.

MLA: Cromie, William J. "Alien Abduction Claims Examined: Signs of Trauma Found." *The Reference Shelf: UFOs,* edited by Micah L. Issitt, Grey House Publishing, 2022, pp. 144-146.

APA: Cromie, W. J. (2022). Alien abduction claims examined signs of trauma found. Micah L. Issitt (Ed.), *The reference shelf: UFOs* (pp. 144-146). Amenia, NY: Grey House Publishing.

Once Upon a Time, Betty and Barney Hill Told a Story That Was Out of This World

By Ray Duckler
Concord Monitor, March 17, 2018

Leon Noel moved carefully toward the row of twisted, sagging apple trees near the Interstate 93 overpass in Lincoln, each step swallowed by two feet of snow.

He pointed with a sweeping motion across the horizon. "There," he said. "That's them."

The trees had been zapped by radiation emitted from an alien craft in 1961. At least that's what Noel had always told his children and then his grandchildren. "They thought it was gospel," Noel said.

That was a family joke. The part about Barney Hill squinting through binoculars and seeing humanoids above this same field, peering from windows like passengers on a plane, was not.

Neither was the part about Hill making a mad dash back to his car on Route 3, screaming in terror to his wife, Betty Hill, that the couple had to leave, fast, or risk capture.

Or the piece about the Hills being taken aboard the craft somewhere near Thornton, then losing all memory for two hours, then arriving at home in Portsmouth as the sun rose and their thoughts were unchained, allowing them to focus, at least partially, on what had happened.

It occurred during a six-hour stretch, beginning near midnight on Sept. 19, 1961, if you believe in that sort of thing.

And don't take my word for it.

Look it up.

"Who knows?" Noel said. "I don't. All I know is something happened."

Noel drives the steam locomotive at Clark's Trading Post. He's lived in Lincoln for nearly 50 years. His hands and smile are gigantic, and his silver hair rises from his head and shoots in different directions, sort of like that craft that Barney and Betty Hill insisted they saw that night 57 years ago.

The yarn is part of the town's landscape, much like those funny-looking apple trees.

As Noel worked his way through the high snow, a 12-year veteran of the Lincoln Police Department pulled over to see what was happening. He declined to give his name.

"I have more than a passing familiarity with what happened," the officer said. "But that doesn't mean I'm a believer."

What about you?

An Alien Concept

The Hills lived in Portsmouth and were just passing through on their way home from Canada. A mixed marriage before those unions were fully accepted, Barney, an African American, died in 1969 from a brain aneurysm at age 46, and Betty, who was white, passed in 2004 from lung cancer at 85.

And yet, like Noel and that steam locomotive, they're forever connected to the Lincoln region. As Noel says, "It was a big thing. My aunt lived here and she was right here, so it was a big thing to talk about. But nothing ever came of it because ..."

Noel's voice trailed off, then he laughed, as though his mind had hit that universal stop sign we all approach. Look one way, and your mind tells you it's not true.

Look the other way, however, and your mind asks, "Why not?"

"There is something out there," Noel says. "For the billions of stars that you look out at with the naked eye at night, we can't be the only flea on the dog."

If what Betty and Barney–the most famous couple with those names since the Flintstones – claimed was true, the 1969 moon landing would be transformed into a walk in the park. But no matter what you believe, the story was out of this world once the media got a hold of it four years after the incident.

A zany-sounding episode, sure, but whiffs of legitimacy–including government scrutiny and hypnosis by a respected Boston physician–followed this like a comet's tail. In fact, even the state added some credibility, planting one of those green historical markers near Indian Head Resort, right there on Route 3, to celebrate the 50th anniversary in 2011.

It reads: "On the night of September 19-20, 1961, Portsmouth, NH couple Betty and Barney Hill experienced a close encounter with an unidentified flying object and two hours of 'lost time' while driving south on Route 3 near Lincoln. They filed an official Air Force Project Blue Book report of a brightly-lit cigar-shaped craft the next day, but were not public with their story until it was leaked in the *Boston Traveler* in 1965."

Then come the words that push you to Google: "This was the first widely-reported UFO abduction report in the United States."

"Somehow Not Human"

In the ensuing years, retired schoolteacher Kathleen Marden, Betty Hill's niece, became obsessed. She's a written a book, compiled a 78-page PDF as part of a presentation and told me by phone from Florida, "My opinion is they did have an encounter with non-human entities. It created an emotional disturbance because it was so close and they had missing time. There were scientists and military people who were interested."

Take everything Marden says, of course, with a grain of cosmic dust. But she no doubt knows more about this topic than anyone in the solar system.

She was 13 when it happened, and says Betty called her sister–Marden's mother–at their home in

> **In memories and then under hypnosis, the Hills revealed that a group of aliens had blocked their car on Route 3 and escorted them aboard.**

Kingston the afternoon after the abduction.

I came home from school during that time frame and heard the end of it," Marden said. "Then we were at the Hill's home a few days later and saw the spots on the car and the watches that had stopped."

Spots on the car? Legend has it that no one could explain what made them on the trunk, or what they were made from. Stopped watches? Yep. Betty and Barney claimed that happened, too.

Early reports said that after the Hills bolted from the field in Lincoln, their car began to vibrate and a tingling sensation passed through their bodies.

That incident also happened in Lincoln, which was the last moment the couple recalled. Their memories returned two hours later in Ashland, about 30 miles away, and it wasn't until four years later that the couple identified the abduction site as Thornton, where an apartment complex now sits.

They quickly reported their experience to the National Investigations Committee on Aerial Phenomena, or NICAP.

In one report, Walter Webb of NICAP filed that "Mr. Hill believed that he was going to be captured 'like a bug in a net.' That is when he knew it was no conventional aircraft he was observing but something alien and enearthly (sic) containing beings of a superior type, beings that were somehow not human."

An Air Intelligence Information Report, prepared by a major at Pease Air Force Base at the same time the Hills say they were abducted, read, "It was revealed that a strange incident occurred on 20 Sept. It is not possible to determine any relationship between these two observations, as the radar observation provides no description.

"Time and distance between the two events could hint at a possible relationship."

Elsewhere, Dr. Benjamin Simon, a renowned psychiatrist from Boston, hypnotized Barney and learned that his severe anxiety was caused by his belief that an abduction had taken place. Betty's description of the event, also made under hypnosis, matched up pretty closely with Barney's.

In memories and then under hypnosis, the Hills revealed that a group of aliens had blocked their car on Route 3 and escorted them aboard. Betty remembered fighting, throwing a punch or a kick, which might explain why her dress was torn. She said they tried to probe her naval, but it hurt so they stopped.

Barney described beings wearing shiny black uniforms with spindly legs, a bulky torso and cat-like eyes.

The Hills tried to keep their experience quiet, but a Boston journalist got a tip in 1965 and ran with the story, even though the Hills declined his requests for an interview.

That initiated a media storm.

"They fled and went to my grandparents' house across the street from me in Kingston," Marden told me. "They knew where Betty and Barney lived, and we had a family meeting on what to do next. There was a lot of media, the phone ringing off the hook."

A Matter of Credibility

The headline, "Aboard a Flying Saucer," teased the Hill story, above a picture of Liz Taylor in a 1966 edition of *Look* magazine.

Then a movie based on the Hill's account called *The UFO Incident* came out in 1975 and starred James Earl Jones as Barney and academy-award winning actress Estelle Parsons as Betty.

Are you getting the idea?

People wanted to believe it. Lots more poked fun at the Hills, calling them nuts or publicity seekers.

Maybe. But these were educated people, a biracial couple far ahead of their time. She was a college graduate and a social worker, he a member of the United States Commission on Civil Rights who was honored by the Northern New England Governor's Conference on Community Action.

They were invited to the 1965 inauguration of President Lyndon Johnson.

And why in the world would a mixed-race couple living in New Hampshire in the early 1960s want to draw attention to themselves in this manner?

Some believed the Hills. Lots more did not.

"People have an agenda to dismiss this sort of thing despite the evidence," Marden told me. "They don't believe in anything. The only thing they will believe is dead bodies and a crashed saucer they can analyze."

That, of course, would help, and by now, if you've made it this far, perhaps you're rolling your eyes, or just plain laughing.

Betty didn't help her cause in later years, claiming she'd seen lots of UFOs flying in groups. Marden felt foolish, telling me she grew angry with her aunt. Only later did Marden forgive her, after learning Betty had a brain tumor, which probably caused her bizarre behavior.

"I had gone with her and sky watchers and I could see helicopters and she was insisting they were moving in unconventional ways," Marden said. "I was disgusted that she was destroying her credibility. It started out with serious investigations and teams of scientists and she went out on her own with crackpot ideas."

By then, however, the story was established. Or at least it made you think.

An Opportunity Lands

The owners of the Notch Express convenience store across from the field in Lincoln take it quite seriously. It's certainly good for business.

Falguni Patel bought the store four years ago and moved the old UFO newspaper clippings from the unisex bathroom to the main area. She sells little flying saucer keychains and green alien dolls with big eyes. There's a mural painted outside showing a skinny alien with a big head.z

"I think it's really true," Patel told me. "There are pretty strong believers in town, so I believe it too. I can see the evidence."

Evidence is in the eye of the beholder. Either way, Lincoln is forever known for the trained bears at Clark's, the train at the Hobo Railroad and the extraterrestrials who some believe appeared in a local field, years before I-93 was built.

The story about those apple trees is fictitious.

The rest?

"All I can say is something happened," Noel said. "What better explanation can you come up with?"

Print Citations

CMS: Duckler, Ray. "Once Upon a Time, Betty and Barney Hill Told a Story That Was Out of This World." In *The Reference Shelf: UFOs,* edited by Micah L. Issitt, 147-151. Amenia, NY: Grey House Publishing, 2022.

MLA: Duckler, Ray. "Once Upon a Time, Betty and Barney Hill Told a Story That Was Out of This World." *The Reference Shelf: UFOs,* edited by Micah L. Issitt, Grey House Publishing, 2022, pp. 147-151.

APA: Duckler, R. (2022). Once upon a time, Betty and Barney Hill told a story that was out of this world. In Micah L. Issitt (Ed.), *The reference shelf: UFOs* (pp. 147-151). Amenia, NY: Grey House Publishing.

Bibliography

Aguilera, Jasmine. "Area 51 Is the Internet's Latest Fascination: Here's Everything to Know About the Mysterious Site." *Time*. July 17, 2019. Retrieved from https://time.com/5627694/area-51-history/.

"Area 51 'Uncensored': Was It UFOs or the USSR?" *NPR*. May 17, 2011. Retrieved from https://www.npr.org/2011/05/17/136356848/area-51-uncensored-was-it-ufos-or-the-ussr.

Bader, Chris D. "The UFO Contact Movement from the 1950s to the Present." *Studies in Popular Culture*. Vol. 17, No. 2. April 1995.

Barnes, Julian, and Helene Cooper. "U.S. Finds No Evidence of Alien Technology in Flying Objects, but Can't Rule It Out, Either." *New York Times*. Sept. 1, 2021. Retrieved from https://www.nytimes.com/2021/06/03/us/politics/ufos-sighting-alien-spacecraft-pentagon.html.

Bowman, Karlyn, and Andrew Rugg. "Public Opinion on Conspiracy Theories." *AEI*. Nov. 2013. Retrieved from https://www.aei.org/wp-content/uploads/2013/11/public-opinion-on-conspiracy-theories_181649218739.pdf?x91208.

Chokshi, Niraj. "The Area 51 'Raid' Is Today. Here's How It Spun Out of Control." *New York Times*. Sept. 14, 2019. Retrieved from https://www.nytimes.com/2019/09/14/us/storm-area-51-raid.html.

Cillizza, Chris. "8 Takeaways from the Government's Big UFO Report." *CNN*. June 28, 2021. Retrieved from https://www.cnn.com/2021/06/27/politics/ufos-uap-extraterrestrial-life/index.html.

David, Leonard. "Experts Weigh In on Pentagon UFO Report." *Scientific American*. June 8, 2021. Retrieved from https://www.scientificamerican.com/article/experts-weigh-in-on-pentagon-ufo-report/.

Davis, Kathleen. "Everything You Need to Know About Sleep Paralysis." *Medical News Today*. May 24, 2017. Retrieved from https://www.medicalnewstoday.com/articles/295039.

Eco, Umberto. *Foucault's Pendulum*. New York: Harcourt, 1988.

Eghigian, Greg. "UFOs and the Boundaries of Science." *Boston Review*. Aug. 4, 2021. Retrieved from https://bostonreview.net/science-nature/greg-eghigian-ufos-and-boundaries-science.

"Harold P. Klein." *NASA*. NASA Ames Hall of Fame. 2021. Retrieved from https://history.arc.nasa.gov/hist_pdfs/bio_klein.pdf.

Hendley, Matthew. "The 'Phoenix Lights' Are No Mystery." *New Times*. Mar. 14, 2014. Retrieved from https://www.phoenixnewtimes.com/news/the-phoenix-lights-are-no-mystery-6661825.

Hubbard, G. Scott. "Astrobiology: Its Origins and Development." *NASA*. Aug. 6,

2008. Retrieved from https://www.nasa.gov/50th/50th_magazine/astrobiology.html.

Kennedy, Courtney, and Arnold Lau. "Most Americans Believe in Intelligent Life Beyond Earth: Few See UFOs as a Major National Security Threat." *Pew Research*. June 30, 2021. Retrieved from https://www.pewresearch.org/fact-tank/2021/06/30/most-americans-believe-in-intelligent-life-beyond-earth-few-see-ufos-as-a-major-national-security-threat/.

Lagrange, Pierre. "A Ghost in the Machine: How Sociology Tries to Explain (Away) American Flying Saucers and European Ghost Rockets, 1946-1947." *Imagining Outer Space*. 2012. Retrieved from https://link.springer.com/chapter/10.1057%2F9780230361362_12.

Loeb, Avi. "What We Can Learn from Studying UFOs." *Scientific American*. June 24, 2021. Retrieved from https://www.scientificamerican.com/article/what-we-can-learn-from-studying-ufos/.

"Majority Say January 6th Was an Attack on Democracy, Quinnipiac University National Poll Finds: About a Quarter of U.S. Still Not Planning to Get Vaccinated." *Quinnipiac Poll*. May 27, 2021. Retrieved from https://poll.qu.edu/images/polling/us/us05272021_ussb63.pdf.

McNally, Richard J. "Explaining 'Memories' of Space Alien Abduction and Past Lives: An Experimental Psychopathology Approach." *Journal of Experimental Psychopathology*. Vol. 3, No. 1, 2012.

McMillian, Tim. "Bob Lazar Says the FBI Raised Him to Seize Area 51's Alien Fuel. The Truth Is Weirder." *Vice*. Nov. 13, 2019. Retrieved from https://www.vice.com/en/article/evjwkw/bob-lazar-says-the-fbi-raided-him-to-seize-area-51s-alien-fuel-the-truth-is-weirder.

Morton, Ella. "The *X-Files* 'I Want to Believe' Poster's Origin Story." *The New Republic*. Dec. 29, 2015. Retrieved from https://newrepublic.com/article/126715/x-files-i-want-believe-posters-origin-story.

Nevett, Joshua. "Storm Area 51: The Joke That Became a 'Possible Humanitarian Disaster.'" *BBC News*. Sept. 13, 2019. Retrieved from https://www.bbc.com/news/world-us-canada-49667295.

Nerlich, Brigitte. "Camille Flammarion: Making Science Popular." *University of Nottingham*. July 22, 2016. Retrieved from https://blogs.nottingham.ac.uk/makingsciencepublic/2016/07/22/camille-flammarion/.

Nir, Sarah Maslin, "With More Time to Look Up, Sightings of UFOs Surged in the Pandemic: 'People Are Reporting These Events.'" *The Baltimore Sun*. Apr. 9, 2021. Retrieved from https://www.baltimoresun.com/news/nation-world/ct-aud-nw-nyt-ufo-sightings-20210409-ztqchqcgzrcflbfedk3c7wjkk4-story.html.

O'Callaghan, Jonathan. "NASA's Curiosity Mars Rover Tests New Way to Search for Alien Life." *New Scientist*. Nov. 1, 2021. Retrieved from https://www.newscientist.com/article/2295603-nasas-curiosity-mars-rover-tests-new-way-to-search-for-alien-life/.

"The Oxcart Story." *Air Force*. Nov. 1, 1994. Retrieved from https://www.airforcemag.com/article/1194oxcart/.

"Project BLUE BOOK–Unidentified Flying Objects." *National Archives*. 2021. Retrieved from https://www.archives.gov/research/military/air-force/ufos.

Rojas, Alejandro. "New Survey Shows Nearly Half of Americans Believe in Aliens." *Huffpost*. Aug. 2, 2017. Retrieved from https://www.huffpost.com/entry/new-survey-shows-nearly-half-of-americans-believe-in_b_59824c11e4b-03d0624b0abe4.

Saad, Lydia. "Americans Skeptical of UFOs but Say Government Knows More." *Gallup Poll*. Sept. 6, 2019. Retrieved from https://news.gallup.com/poll/266441/americans-skeptical-ufos-say-government-knows.aspx.

___. "Do Americans Believe in UFOs?" *Gallup*. Aug. 20, 2021. Retrieved from https://news.gallup.com/poll/350096/americans-believe-ufos.aspx.

___. "Larger Minority in U.S. Says Some UFOs Are Alien Spacecraft." *Gallup*. Aug. 20, 2021. Retrieved from https://news.gallup.com/poll/353420/larger-minority-says-ufos-alien-spacecraft.aspx.

Salisbury, David F. "Scientific Panel Concludes Some UFO Evidence Worthy of Study." *Stanford*. June 22, 1998. Retrieved from https://news.stanford.edu/pr/98/980629ufostudy.html.

Scharf, Caleb A. "The First Alien." *Scientific American*. Nov. 23, 2019. Retrieved from https://blogs.scientificamerican.com/life-unbounded/the-first-alien/.

Scoles, Sarah. "How UFO Sightings Became an American Obsession." *Wired*. Mar. 3, 2020. Retrieved from https://www.wired.com/story/how-ufo-sightings-became-an-american-obsession/.

Shane, Leo III. "Trust in the Military Is Dropping Significantly, New Survey Suggests." *Military Times*. Mar. 10, 2021. Retrieved from https://www.militarytimes.com/news/pentagon-congress/2021/03/10/trust-in-the-military-is-dropping-significantly-new-survey-suggests/.

Shostak, Seth. "Harvard's Avi Loeb Things We Should Study UFOs—and He's Not Wrong." *Scientific American*. July 29, 2021. Retrieved from https://www.scientificamerican.com/article/harvard-rsquo-s-avi-loeb-thinks-we-should-study-ufos-mdash-and-he-rsquo-s-not-wrong/.

"UFOs Eyed Nukes, Ex-Air Force Personnel Say." *CNN*. Sept. 27, 2010. Retrieved from https://news.blogs.cnn.com/2010/09/27/ufos-showed-interest-in-nukes-ex-air-force-personnel-say/.

"UFO Report: US Finds No Explanation for Sightings." *BBC News*. June 25, 2021. Retrieved from https://www.bbc.com/news/world-us-canada-57619755.

Weiss, Josh. "New Docu-Series Explores How Betty and Barney Hill Changed UFO Culture with Their Famous Story of Alien Abduction." *Syfy*. Aug. 25, 2021. Retrieved from https://www.syfy.com/syfy-wire/betty-barney-hill-ufo-showtime.

Zielinski, Sarah. "The Great Moon Hoax Was Simply a Sign of Its Time." *Smithsonian*. July 2, 2015. Retrieved from https://www.smithsonianmag.com/smithsonian-institution/great-moon-hoax-was-simply-sign-its-time-180955761/.

Websites

Center for UFO Studies (CUFOS)

www.cufos.com

The Center for UFO Studies is a small research organization started by individuals who worked on the Project Blue Book program initiated by the Pentagon in the early 1950s. CUFOS invites participation by scientists, academics, and researchers involved in any field connected to UFO studies. The organization's website provides a wide variety of articles on UFO sightings, researchers in the field, and links to other resources for individuals interested in learning about UFOs and allows visitors to report their own UFO sightings.

The International UFO Congress

www.ufocongress.com

The International UFO Congress is a promotional organization that organizes an annual meeting of UFO enthusiasts. Typically, meetings of the congress will feature interviews and speeches with individuals who have experienced contact with aliens or UFOs and covers issues such as UFO sightings, crash sites and historical UFO studies, and alien abduction. The organization is owned by Out of This World Media and Events and, in 2021, hosted a virtual only event.

Mutual UFO Network (MUFON)

www.mufon.com

The Mutual UFO Network is a true mainstream UFO enthusiast's organization. The nonprofit organization cooperates in studying local UFO sightings. The organization's website allows visitors to post UFO sightings, along with video or photographic evidence, and essentially crowd-sources information on UFO incidents. The organization also provides links to local and national news on UFO sightings, interviews with UFO experiencers, and researchers studying UFO sightings and related issues.

The NASA Astrobiology Institute (NAI)

Nai.nasa.gov

NASA's Astrobiology Institute was, until 2021, the branch of NASA focused on detecting and studying extraterrestrial life. The NAI website contains links to articles about astrobiological research and articles discussing careers in astrobiology and other space science fields. The NAI also has links to a number of seminars, educational programs, and other resources of interest in students and professionals in the astrobiology field. The NAI also provides recent news from scientists and programs involved with the NAI through various universities and private research organizations.

National Aeronautics and Space Administration (NASA)
www.nasa.gov

The National Aeronautics and Space Administration (NASA) is the premier US government agency with authority over space exploration and the development of space technology. Established in 1958, NASA manages a broad range of resources in many different fields, supporting the development of new tools and technology, supporting educational programs in astrophysics, aeronautics, and many other subfields of space science, and research to better understand the earth and its connection to the broader universe. NASA also manages US facilities focused on space science research and observatories for observing cosmic phenomena.

National UFO Reporting Center
www.NUFORC.org

The National UFO Reporting Center is, as described, an organization that invites individuals to report UFO sightings and other extraterrestrial experiences. The organization operates a telephone hotline, allows digital reporting, and maintains a database of other sightings, and cases involving aliens or unidentified phenomena. Originally established in 1974, the organization seeks to build a database of experience reports, rather than to advocate for belief or skepticism. Coverage of incidents is factual, focusing on reporting details rather than providing interpretation or evaluations of accurate. The organization also provides a convenient "noteworthy cases" feature highlighting the most interesting recent UFO reports.

Search for Extraterrestrial Intelligence (SETI)
www.seti.org

Search for Extraterrestrial Intelligence (SETI) is an organization encompassing a large number of scientific programs around the world focused on searching for and detecting signs of extraterrestrial life. SETI programs include a variety of scanning and observational programs utilizing various types of technology to search for possible alien vessels, or communication. The SETI Center's website provides a variety of articles discussing the scientific search for life outside the solar system, astrobiology, and explaining some of the technology and studies looking for signs of extraterrestrial communication.

Index